Write soon!

MW01254369

Write soon!

A Beginning Text
for ESL Writers

Eileen Prince
Northeastern University

HEINLE & HEINLE PUBLISHERS
A Division of Wadsworth, Inc.
Boston, Massachusetts 02116

Library of Congress Cataloging-in-Publication Data

Prince, Eileen.
    Write Soon! A Beginning Text for ESL Writers / Eileen Prince
        p.   cm.
    ISBN 0-8384-3389-8
    1. English language — Textbooks for foreign speakers. 2. English
language — Rhetoric. I. Title.
PE1128.P735 1990
808'.042 — dc20   89-2718
                                                                                    CIP

Copyright © 1990 by Heinle & Heinle Publishers, a division of
Wadsworth, Inc.

All rights reserved. No part of this book may be reproduced or
transmitted in any form or by any means, electronic or mechanical,
including photocopying, recording, or any information storage and
retrieval system, without permission in writing from the Publisher.

Photo Credits

Page ii: *Top left*, Eileen Prince; *right*, © *Financial Times*/Gamma-Liaison; *bottom left*, The Bettmann Archive. **Page 1:** Eileen Prince. **Page 8:** Eileen Prince. **Page 11:** *Left* and *right*, Eileen Prince. **Page 20:** *Top right*, © John Chiasson/Gamma-Liaison; *bottom left* and *right*, Sona Doran. **Page 21:** © Robert Alexander/Gamma-Liaison. **Page 70:** Sona Doran. **Page 71:** *Above* and *below left*, Eileen Prince; *top right*, Sona Doran. **Page 127:** Russ Sparkman/Northeastern University. **Page 142:** The Bettmann Archive. **Page 170:** *Top left*, Eileen Prince; *above right*, © Mark Reinstein/Gamma-Liaison; *below right*, © Lochon/Gamma-Liaison. **Page 172:** *Left*, Eric Liebowitz; *right*, © *Financial Times*/Gamma-Liaison. **Page 195:** *Above left*, Eileen Prince; *below right*, Sona Doran. **Page 203:** Eileen Prince. **Page 217:** *Left*, Eileen Prince; *right*, Sona Doran. **Page 219:** *Above* and *below left*, The Bettmann Archive; *top right*, Sona Doran.

This book was set in New Caledonia by V & M Graphics,
printed and bound by R.R. Donnelley & Sons.
The cover was printed by Lehigh Press Lithographers

Printing: 3 4 5 6 7   Year: 3 4 5 6

Printed in the U.S.A.

ISBN 0-02-396801-X

To Katie,
whose tragic disability
has made me aware of what a wonderful
and necessary gift language is.

Acknowledgments

I would like to express my gratitude to the staff and teachers at the English Language Center of Northeastern University for providing a supportive atmosphere in which I was able to write and try out this book. In particular, I wish to thank Judith DeFilippo, Paul Everett, and Eleanor Lander for trying out earlier versions of many of the lessons and for giving me constructive feedback. A special, warm thanks is due to Karen F. Colby-DeMattos, friend and colleague, who graciously agreed to read the entire manuscript and make suggestions for revisions. Thanks for comments and suggestions also go to the anonymous reviewers provided by Macmillan, and to Mary Jane Peluso and Maggie Barbieri for encouraging me to submit and, ultimately, complete this text.

This space also provides me with a chance to thank my family. Thanks to my children—Deborah, Suzanne, Penelope, and Katherine Nam; they inspired me to want to succeed. Thanks to my father, the late David J. Prince, who spent long hours with me during my childhood making me aware of the fun that language and stories can be. Finally, thanks to my mother, Margaret Prince, for providing the nurturing childhood that enabled me to grow to become what I am today.

Contents

CHAPTER **4** *Describing People and*
What They Are Doing   70

CHAPTER 5 *Writing About the Future*

CHAPTER **8** *Using Comparison and Contrast*   169

CHAPTER 9 *Giving Advice*   194

CHAPTER **10**   *Writing About the Past*   216

Introduction

WHY THIS BOOK?

This beginning writing text is intended for late teenage and adult learners, people whose cognitive abilities are greater than their linguistic abilities in English. The tasks it provides gradually increase in difficulty and are meant to set students on a path that will prepare them for the types of writing they will be called upon to do in an academic or business setting.

This book answers the need for a text that can provide all of the material that is needed for an elementary ESL writing course. As a teacher and administrator, I have observed that teachers often assign a grammar text for a writing course because their students' most apparent problem is with writing correct sentences. They then provide the writing "text" themselves, often using a workshop approach with pair work and teacher feedback. At the elementary level, this approach may leave both teacher and student floundering. This book provides both the grammar and the writing text that are needed in a course for elementary ESL writers. It meets the following needs:

1. It provides the reference grammar and exercises that teachers want in a writing text.
2. It provides models for students to refer to in writing and editing their own work and that of their peers.
3. It introduces different types of organization, even at this elementary level.

4. It has a process approach to writing.
5. It is interesting. The topics are varied. Students write about themselves or their experiences and topics of general interest. There are visuals and pair activities in every chapter.
6. It recognizes that writing is not "frozen speech" but rather the product of conscious or monitored work for which rules or guidelines must be given.

Pair work is central to this text. There are three reasons for my deciding to exploit this type of activity. First, not all writing classes are small enough to permit the teacher to interact with each student during every class. Pair activities free the teacher to work with individual students or groups on their particular areas of difficulty. Second, pair work provides the fledgling ESL writer with an immediate audience. Partners are able to ask each other for more information during the writing process and to share their interest in a topic. This is quite different from a teacher looking at a final product and then asking about it. Teachers simply cannot be with every student at the same time to perform this immediate audience function. Third, the practice that students get in editing and asking questions about their partners' work is transferable. In my experience teaching writing, it is easier for students to learn to expand and edit their own work after they have had a lot of practice editing the work of others. They become better able to view a piece objectively after they have become accustomed to reading their partners' work with an eye toward revising and editing.

THEORETICAL PERSPECTIVE

This is first and foremost a *writing* text. Writing, in a language with a rich literature and with use of the written word for academic and other communication, is not merely speech that has been translated into graphic symbols. It is a form that is — although rooted in speech — independent, with its own rules of both grammar and discourse.

Writing should be, more than any other aspect of language, a *monitored activity*. Therefore, it is important to aid students early on in monitoring their writing. This monitoring should be done at both the level of grammar and mechanics and the level of organization of paragraphs and essays. Writing is a process; however, we are ultimately concerned with product. Therefore, students of writing must be presented with models toward which they can aim. It is important for them to know what is considered acceptable, native-speaker writing.

Adult learners, even at the elementary level, are in fact capable of beginning formal writing. Because their cognitive abilities are far greater than their linguistic level in English, the task is to tap the former while not taxing the latter too greatly. In this text, students are given careful guidance to enable them to produce the formal written form of the language they are currently capable of.

To the Teacher

Each chapter provides teaching material for at least five hours of class work at the high-elementary or low-intermediate level. For a true beginning class or for a class that is using this text for a combination grammar and writing course, plan on ten hours per chapter, at least at first. Depending on the class, you may be able to decrease the number of class hours per chapter after the first few. In no case would I recommend spending more than ten hours on a chapter. Even if your class seems to require more time, go on to the next chapter. Later, go back to the last chapter's "More Writing" section and use some of the topics there to repeat the various processes of the chapter. Students tend to get bored if they spend too much time on one unit of work. One purpose of the "More Writing" section is to allow for recycling without discouragement. Students can be presented with a review writing task in the guise of a new topic.

Here is a suggested daily schema for each chapter in a high-elementary or low-intermediate writing class that meets one hour a day, five days a week, as part of an intensive program.

Day One: Begin with section 1, "Pre-Writing." Continue with section 2, "Writing Sentences." Assign study of section 3, "Grammar," for homework. Ask students to do some of the grammar exercises at home.

Day Two: Have students go over selected grammar exercises. Collect others. Move on to section 4, "Editing." Allow at least half an hour for this activity. Students will be getting grammar practice here, because this section asks them to review the grammar section. Assign study of section 5, "Connectors and Transitions," for homework.

Day Three: Go over section 5 in class. Devote the major part of the class time to section 6, "Getting Ready to Write a Paragraph." For homework assign extra grammar exercises if you wish. More importantly, ask students to begin thinking about the paragraph they will be writing in section 7, "Writing a Paragraph." You may want to ask them to practice freewriting or brainstorming at home.

Day Four: Have students do section 8, "Expanding Your Paragraph," in class. If time permits, ask them to do the revising part of section 9,

"Revising and Editing." Their homework assignment is to begin revising and editing their own writing in anticipation of work with their partner.

Day Five: Have students do section 9, "Revising and Editing." Use as much time as is available to allow them to start writing their final drafts. Assign completion of the final draft for homework.

You may notice that section 10, "More Writing," has been left out of this schema. This omission is deliberate. For me, this section has two purposes. It is meant to provide review activities for recycling at a later date. It is also meant to provide extra work for those students who are able to move through the other sections of the chapter more quickly than their classmates. One advantage of this text is that it allows you to individualize instruction for groups of students. Some can move more quickly and others can move more slowly. The provision for work with a partner allows you to work with individuals and small groups as necessary.

The schema I have provided assumes that you will be using all parts of each chapter. However, this is not necessary. Just as students have different styles of learning, teachers have preferred styles of teaching. As a trainer and evaluator of teachers, I have learned that one of the most important components of good instruction is for teachers to believe in and feel comfortable with their teaching styles. If you prefer to spend more time than I have suggested going over grammar and mechanics, by all means do so. If you prefer to concentrate on the writing process and to de-emphasize the grammar exercises, please follow your inclinations. Use whatever approach you feel comfortable with, but please remember that some of your students may have different preferences, too. If certain students seem to work better by studying or reviewing rules before taking the plunge into writing, let them try it. If others prefer to get on with the process, allow them the freedom to do so. The unique feature of this text is that it provides you with the latitude to follow your own basic teaching style while respecting those students who may do better with a different learning style. Experiment—see what works for you and for them.

Finally, let me say something about the models that are provided in each chapter. They are there because many learners expect and/or need them; however, they are not intended to provide an absolute standard by which student work is to be measured. Writing in a foreign language, although a monitored activity, proceeds developmentally. Although the editing activities in each chapter allow students to focus their monitors on particular points, it is unrealistic to expect the students to produce flawless essays, especially at this point in their writing careers. Expect and allow room for mistakes. Encourage your students to aim for content as well as accuracy. Let the models serve as goals to be reached eventually, but make it clear that this time is in the future. Your students will become better writers if they are allowed room for growth.

TO THE STUDENT

This book will help you begin the process of learning to write essays in English. However, most of the responsibility for your writing is yours. I hope that you will work with your teacher and classmates to achieve this goal. I hope that this book and the activities it provides will make your work interesting.

You will do a lot of your writing in this book, but you will need paper for your longer assignments and essays. I suggest that you use lined loose-leaf paper. You will also need something to write with. Ask your teacher whether he or she prefers that you write with a pen or a pencil. Whatever materials you use, enjoy yourself. I hope that this book makes learning to write a pleasure.

E. P.

CHAPTER 1

Describing People

Topic: Describing yourself and other people

Rhetorical Focus: One topic per paragraph

Mechanical Focus: Capitals, periods, commas, and question marks; paragraph form

Grammatical Focus: Subjects; simple present tense of *to be*; possessive adjectives

Connectors and Transitions: *and*

1 PRE-WRITING: DIFFERENT KINDS OF LETTERS

Read these sentences about Linda.

1. My name is Linda.
2. I am from Florida.
3. I am a teacher.
4. My hair is black, and my eyes are brown.

Different Kinds of Letters

	Capital Letter	Small Letter		
Printed:	A	a	B	b

	Capital Letter	Small Letter		
Hand–Printed:	A	a	B	b

	Capital Letter	Small Letter		
Script:	𝒜	a	ℬ	b

Printed:	C	c	D	d	E	e	F	f
Hand–Printed:	C	c	D	d	E	e	F	f
Script:	C	c	D	d	E	e	F	f

Printed:	G	g	H	h	I	i	J	j
Hand–Printed:	G	g	H	h	I	i	J	j
Script:	G	g	H	h	I	i	J	j

Printed:	K	k	L	l	M	m	N	n
Hand–Printed:	K	k	L	l	M	m	N	n
Script:	K	k	L	l	M	m	N	n

Printed:	O	o	P	p	Q	q	R	r
Hand–Printed:	O	o	P	p	Q	q	R	r
Script:	O	o	P	p	Q	q	R	r

Printed:	S	s	T	t	U	u	V	v
Hand–Printed:	S	s	T	t	U	u	V	v
Script:	S	s	T	t	U	u	V	v

Printed:	W	w	X	x	Y	y	Z	z
Hand–Printed:	W	w	X	x	Y	y	Z	z
Script:	W	w	X	x	Y	y	Z	z

Period	Comma	Question Mark	Exclamation Mark
.	,	?	!

Read Linda's sentences on page 1 again. Here are the same sentences in hand-printed and handwritten letters.

1. My name is Linda.
   My name is Linda.

2. I am from Florida.
   I am from Florida.

3. I am a teacher.
   I am a teacher.

4. My hair is black, and my eyes are brown.
   My hair is black, and my eyes are brown.

Now, work with your partner to fill in each blank using script letters. The first one is done for you.

1. Each sentence begins with a *capital letter.*
2. Each sentence ends with a _____.
3. The first word after a comma begins with a _____.
4. The names of people and places begin with a _____.

2 WRITING SENTENCES

EXERCISE 1

Follow steps 1, 2, and 3 for each group of letters and words.

1. Match each letter on the left with the word on the right that begins with the same letter. *Pay attention to the difference between small letters and capital letters.*

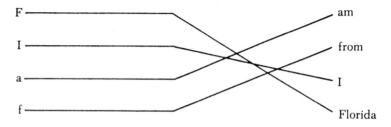

2. Next, using script, write the word next to the letter.

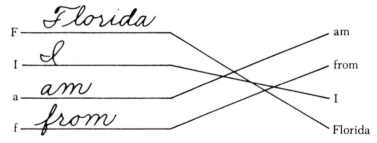

3. Finally, put each group of words in the correct order to make a sentence, and write the sentence in the space provided.

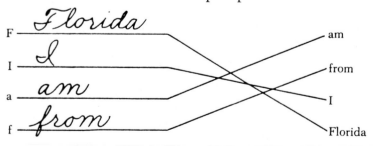

i _____ is

L _____ your

t _____ Linda

y _____ teacher

J _____ from

A _____ John

f _____ is

i _____ Australia

C _____ are

T _____ Canada

f _____ students

a _____ from

s _____ Those

i _____ blond

H _____ hair

b _____ His

h _____ is

EXERCISE 2

Read the sentences about Linda in section 1 again. Then, write sentences about yourself.

Who am I?

_____

_____

_____

_____

_____

_____

_____

_____

_____

EXERCISE 3

Look at the photograph of Linda in section 1. Then, answer the questions about her in the space provided. Use sentences. Begin each sentence with a capital lettter. End each sentence with a period. The first sentence is done for you.

1. What is her name?

   Her name is Linda.

2. Where is she from?

   _____

3. Is she a teacher or a student?

_____

4. What color is her hair?

_____

5. What color are her eyes?

_____

3 GRAMMAR

A SUBJECTS

In most English sentences, the person or thing that the sentence is about is called the subject. In simple declarative sentences, the subject usually comes before the verb. It consists of a pronoun or a noun plus any words that modify that pronoun or noun.

EXERCISE 1

Here are some sentences about Linda. Underline the subject in each of the sentences. The first one is done for you.

1. <u>Linda</u> is a teacher.
2. She is from Florida.
3. Her eyes are brown.
4. Richard is her student.
5. Those students are in her class.
6. Her office is in a tall building.
7. Her students are from different countries.
8. Her classroom is in a small building.

EXERCISE 2

Here are some sentences about John. Underline the subject in each of the sentences.

1. John is a student.
2. He is from Australia.
3. Ping is his teacher.
4. John's hair is blond.
5. His eyes are blue.

B THE SIMPLE PRESENT TENSE OF *TO BE*

In English, the verb agrees with the subject of the sentence. Here are some sentences that contain the simple present forms of the verb *to be*.

Subject	*to be*	Rest of the Sentence
I	am	a teacher.
You	are	a student.
He	is	from Lebanon.
She	is	Chinese.
It	is	a nice day.
We	are	students.
You	are	teachers.
They	are	from Australia.

EXERCISE 3

**Fill in each blank with the correct present form of the verb *to be*.
The first one is done for you.**

1. I am a student. I __*am*__ not a teacher.

2. Linda is not a student. She _____ a teacher.

3. Where are you from? I _____ from Canada.

4. It _____ a beautiful day, and we _____ happy.

5. Are you students or teachers? We _____ students.

6. Where is John from? He _____ from Australia.

C POSSESSIVE ADJECTIVES

Possessive adjectives modify nouns by telling who the nouns belong to. They
are like pronouns. They refer back to a noun or pronoun. This noun or
pronoun is called the *antecedent.*

Antecedent	Possessive Adjective
Ping is a teacher.	*His* native language is Chinese.
Rosa is a student.	*Her* history teacher is Ping.

**Look at the following sentences. The possessive adjectives are circled.
The antecedents are underlined. There is an arrow from each
possessive adjective to the antecedent.**

1. I am in a French class. (My) classroom is small.

2. You are my classmate. (Your) name is Noriko.

3. Linda is a teacher. (Her) office is in a tall building.

4. <u>John</u> is a student. (His) native country is Australia. English is his native language.

5. That is not Linda's <u>class</u>. (Its) teacher is Ping.

6. <u>We</u> are from Venezuela. (Our) native language is Spanish.

7. <u>You</u> are students in my class. (Your) teacher is Mary.

8. <u>They</u> are in my class. (Their) native language is Chinese.

EXERCISE 4

Fill in each blank with the correct possessive adjective. The antecedent is underlined. The first one is done for you.

1. <u>I</u> am a student. _____*My*_____ native language is Greek.

2. <u>We</u> are in a history class. _____ teacher is Ping.

3. <u>Mary</u> is an English teacher. _____ office is in a small building.

4. <u>Those students</u> are in Mary's class. _____ native language is Arabic.

5. <u>The classroom</u> is empty. _____ door is locked.

6. <u>You</u> are from Japan. _____ native language is Japanese.

7. <u>Ping</u> is a history teacher. _____ office is in a tall building.

4 EDITING

Look at the photographs of Linda in section 1 and John in section 3. Cross out the sentences that are not about them.

Linda is a teacher.   John is a student.
She is from Florida.   He is from Australia.
~~My hair is short.~~   His hair is blond.
Her hair is long.   It is a nice day.
Her eyes are brown.   His eyes are blue.

Now, look at these pictures. Cross out the sentences that are not about the picture that they are under.

Rosa and John are students.   This is our class.
They are in a history class.   We are in our room.
Math is Rosa's favorite subject.   Our teacher is not here.
They are in Boston.   His hair is brown.
Ping is their teacher.

5 CONNECTORS AND TRANSITIONS

AND

You can combine simple sentences by using the conjunction *and*. Here are some examples.

1. My hair is black.

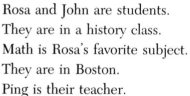

My eyes are brown.

My hair is black, and my eyes are brown.

2. Ping is a history teacher.

Linda is an English teacher.

Ping is a history teacher, and Linda is an English teacher.

Fill in the blanks.

1. There is a _____ before *and* in the new sentence.

2. Only the first word of the new sentence begins with a _____

   letter.

EXERCISE

**Combine each pair of sentences using *and*. Write your new sentence.
The first one is done for you.**

1. Rosa is from Venezuela.

   Ping is from China.

   Rosa is from Venezuela, and Ping is from China.

2. Rosa's hair is brown.

   Her eyes are brown.

   _____
   _____
   _____

3. I am a student.

   You are a teacher.

   _____
   _____
   _____

4. It is warm.

}

The sky is blue.

_____

_____

_____

5. We are in an English class.

}

They are in a history class.

_____

_____

_____

6 GETTING READY TO WRITE A PARAGRAPH

Make a list of questions to ask your partner about himself or herself, and write them in the space provided. Your partner will also make a list of questions to ask you. Be sure to begin your questions with a capital letter and to end them with a question mark (?).

Questions for My Partner

_____

_____

_____

_____

_____

_____

_____

Now, take turns reading your questions to one another. Write your answers in the space provided. Be sure to answer the questions with sentences. Be sure to begin your sentences with capital letters and to end them with periods.

Answers to My Partner's Questions

_____
_____
_____
_____
_____
_____
_____
_____
_____
_____
_____
_____
_____
_____
_____

7 WRITING A PARAGRAPH

The sentences about Linda in section 1 are all about the same topic. They can be put together to make a *paragraph*.

Proper Paragraph Form

Left–
hand
margin

Indent for the
first sentence.

My name is Linda. I am from

Florida. I am a teacher. My

Skip
every
other
line.

hair is black, and my eyes

are brown.

EXERCISE

Look at the answers that you wrote to your partner's questions. Are all of them about the same topic (that is, about you)? Can you make them into a paragraph?

Write a paragraph about yourself. Use a piece of lined paper. Be sure to use a left-hand margin and to indent for the first sentence. Begin each sentence with a capital letter, and end each sentence with a period. Be sure to use commas if you need them.

8 EXPANDING YOUR PARAGRAPH

Read your partner's paragraph. Let your partner read your paragraph.

Is there more information that you want about your partner? Write more questions for your partner to answer. Write them in your partner's book. Let your partner write more questions in your book. Write answers to your partner's questions.

My Partner's Questions

_____

_____

_____

_____

_____

My Answers

_____

_____

_____

_____

_____

_____

_____

_____

_____

9 REVISING AND EDITING

A REVISING

Read the answers that you wrote in section 8. Are any of them about the same topic as your paragraph? Do you want to add them to your paragraph?

On a clean piece of lined paper, rewrite your paragraph with the new information that you want to add.

B EDITING

Read your partner's paragraph. Let your partner read your paragraph. Check your partner's paragraph for the following:

1. Is the paragraph form correct? (Look at page 15.)
2. Is the sentence form correct? (Review section 2.)
3. Are the forms of the verb *to be* correct? Underline all forms of the verb *to be*. Is each the correct form for its subject? (Review section 3B.)
4. Are the possessive adjectives correct? Circle the possessive adjectives. Can you find their antecedents? Are the forms of the possessive adjectives correct? (Review section 3C.)

Give back your partner's paragraph. Look at your paragraph. Copy it again with any corrections that are necessary. Give your finished paragraph to your teacher.

10   MORE WRITING

Follow your teacher's instructions, or work on this section on your own if you have time.

1. With your partner, draw a picture of another person. Then, work with your partner to write a one-paragraph description of the person.
2. Bring a photograph of a friend or relative to class. Write a one-paragraph description of this person.
3. Find several pictures of people in a newspaper or magazine. Bring them to class. Choose *one* of the pictures. Write a one-paragraph description of the person in the picture. Then, show *all* of the pictures to your classmates. Let them read your paragraph. Can they guess which picture you wrote about?

CHAPTER 2

Supporting Generalizations

Topic: Cities, seasons, and favorite things

Rhetorical Focus: Supporting generalizations

Mechanical Focus: Capital letters; commas

Grammatical Focus: Pronouns; countable and uncountable nouns

Connectors and Transitions: *but*; *because*; *for example*

1 PRE-WRITING: FINDING THE TOPIC OF A PARAGRAPH

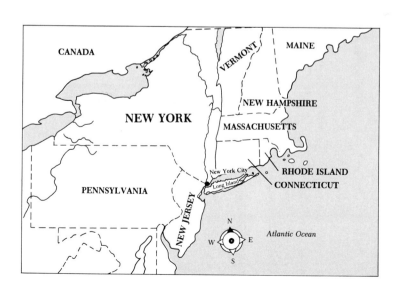

Read the following paragraph about New York.

New York is an important city. It is a major port. Its population is almost eight million. Many foreign embassies are in New York. It is not the capital of the United States, but it is the center of many activities. For example, it is the financial and fashion center of the country.

The first sentence tells what the paragraph is about. It is called the *topic sentence*. All of the other sentences *support* this sentence. They tell why New York is an important city in the United States.

Now, read the following paragraph about trees.

Trees are useful and beautiful during every season of the year. They are beautiful in the spring because their leaves are green. In the summer, trees are good protection on hot days. In the autumn, their red, orange, and yellow leaves are like a painting. Even in the winter, their bare branches are reminders of the beautiful days of spring.

What is the topic sentence of this paragraph? Write it in the space provided.

_____

_____

Now, read the following paragraph about summer.

In the summer, the days are long, and the sky is usually blue. At the beach, the sand is soft, and the water is warm. Students are happy because they are on vacation. Summer is my favorite season.

What is the topic sentence of this paragraph? Write it in the space provided.

_____

_____

Is the topic sentence always the first sentence in a paragraph?

Yes, it is. _____   No, it isn't. _____

2 WRITING SENTENCES

Complete the following sentences by filling in the blanks. Then, copy the complete sentence in the space provided. Be sure to begin each sentence with a capital letter and to end each sentence with a period. If you use the name of a person, city, or country, begin the name with a capital letter.

1. _____ is my favorite season.

_____

_____

2. _____ is a(n) _____ city.

_____

_____

3. _____ are _____

_____

3 GRAMMAR

A PRONOUNS

Here is the paragraph about New York again. The pronouns and possessive

adjectives are underlined, and their antecedents are circled. Arrows connect
the pronouns (or possessive adjectives) and their antecedents.

(New York) is an important city. It is a major port. Its

population is almost eight million. Many foreign embassies

are in (New York.) It is not the capital of the United States,

but it is the center of many activities. For example, it is the

financial and fashion center of the country.

EXERCISE 1

**Reread the paragraph about trees. Underline the pronouns and
possessive adjectives. Circle their antecedents. Draw arrows to
connect them.**

Trees are useful and beautiful during every season of the

year. They are beautiful in the spring because their leaves are

green. In the summer, trees are good protection on hot days.

In the autumn, their red, orange, and yellow leaves are like a

painting. Even in the winter, their bare branches are

reminders of the beautiful days of spring.

B COUNTABLE AND UNCOUNTABLE NOUNS

Some English nouns are countable, and others are uncountable. Countable nouns have a singular form and a plural form. Usually, the plural form ends in -s.

Singular	Plural
center	centers
day	days
port	ports
season	seasons
tree	trees

Nouns that end in the letter *y* preceded by a consonant follow a special rule. They form the plural by changing the *y* to *i* and adding -es.

Singular	Plural
activity	activities
city	cities
country	countries
embassy	embassies

Nouns that end in the letters *x*, *ch*, *sh*, *s*, and *z* form their plurals by adding -es.

Singular	Plural
beach	beaches
branch	branches
class	classes

There are some other special spelling rules for forming plurals. For example, some nouns that end in the letter *f* form their plurals by changing the *f* to *v* and adding *-es*.

Singular	Plural
leaf	leaves
scarf	scarves

EXERCISE 2

Rewrite each sentence so that it is about the subjects in parentheses. Make all other necessary changes. The first sentence is done for you.

1. New York is an important port. (New York and London)

   New York and London are important ports.

2. Spring is a colorful season. (Spring and autumn)

3. Shanghai is a big city. (Shanghai and Lagos)

4. Ottawa is the capital of its country. (Ottawa and Paris)

5. Brazil is a big country. (Brazil and Canada)

6. Arabic is an important language. (Arabic and Japanese)

_____

_____

7. Waikiki is a beautiful beach. (Waikiki and the Costa del Sol)

_____

_____

8. That is a beautiful leaf. (Those)

_____

_____

C UNCOUNTABLE NOUNS

Uncountable nouns only have a singular form. They usually refer to things
that people think of as a *mass* or an abstract concept. Here are some
examples.

>   hair   population   sand   water   weather

Because uncountable nouns only have a singular form, they always take the
form of the verb that goes with the pronoun *it*.

EXERCISE 3

**Fill in each blank in the following paragraph with the correct form of
the verb *to be*.**

> Fruit _____ very colorful. Bananas _____ yellow with
>
> some green and brown. Grapes _____ different colors. Some
>
> _____ green, some _____ red, some _____ purple, and
>
> some _____ almost black. Apples _____ also different
>
> colors. Their skin _____ red, yellow, or green, and their
>
> flesh _____ bright white. The fruit section of a supermarket
>
> _____ a very colorful place.

4 EDITING

In the following groups of sentences, the topic sentence is given first.
It is underlined. Under it, there is a list of sentences. All of them
support the topic sentence except for one. Cross out the sentence in
each group that does not support the topic sentence. Then, tell why
that sentence does not support the topic sentence. The first one is
done for you.

London is an important city.
It is the capital of England.
~~It is in Europe.~~
It is a commercial port.

The fact that London is in Europe does not support the idea that it is an

important city. Many European cities are not important.

Dogs are good pets.
They are friendly animals.
They are loyal to people.
They are playful.
Cats are good pets, too.

_____

_____

_____

Autumn is my favorite season.
The colorful leaves on the trees are beautiful.
Winter is my brother's favorite season.
The weather is cool and nice.
School is open.

_____

_____

_____

5 CONNECTORS AND TRANSITIONS

A BUT

You can combine simple sentences that contrast with each other by using the conjunction *but.* Here are some examples.

1. New York is not the capital of the United States.

   It is the center of many activities.

   New York is not the capital of the United States, but it is the center of many activities

2. Winter is very cold.

   It is my favorite season.

   Winter is very cold, but it is my favorite season.

Fill in the blanks.

1. There is a _____ before *but* in the new sentence.

2. Only the first word of the new sentence begins with a _____ .

EXERCISE 1

Combine each pair of sentences to make one sentence. Connect sentences that contrast with *but*. Connect sentences that do not contrast with *and*. The first two are done for you.

1. Cats are beautiful.

   Dogs are my favorite animals.

   Cats are beautiful, but dogs are

   my favorite animals.

2. The sky is usually blue in the summer.

   It is usually warm.

   The sky is usually blue in the
   summer, and it is usually warm.

3. Autumn is Fred's favorite season.

   Spring is Linda's favorite season.

   _____

   _____

   _____

   _____

   _____

4. Hawaii is a group of islands in the Pacific Ocean.

   It is a part of the United States.

   _____

   _____

   _____

   _____

   _____

5. Apples are delicious.

   They are good for you.

   _____

   _____

   _____

   _____

   _____

EXERCISE 2

Write about your favorite season or your favorite food. Write two sentences that contain *and*.

1. _____

_____

2. _____

_____

How are you and your partner different? Write two sentences that contain *but*.

3. _____

_____

4. _____

_____

B *BECAUSE*

You can combine simple sentences that show cause and effect by using *because*. Here are some examples.

1. The students are happy.

   They are on vacation.

   The students are happy because they are on vacation.

2. Dogs are good pets.

   They are friendly.

   Dogs are good pets because they are friendly.

Now, answer these questions.

1. Is there a comma in the new sentence? _____

2. Which word of the new sentence begins with a capital letter?

_____

EXERCISE 3

Combine each pair of sentences to make one sentence. Connect sentences that show cause and effect with *because*. Connect sentences that contrast with *but*. Connect other sentences with *and*. The first two are done for you.

1. Summer is my favorite season.

   It is warm.

   Summer is my favorite season

   because it is warm.

2. Everything is beautiful in the spring.

   It is not my favorite season.

   Everything is beautiful in the

   spring, but it is not my favorite

   season.

3. Cats are good pets.

   They are quiet.

   _____

   _____

   _____

   _____

   _____

4. Paris is an important city.

It is the capital of France.

_____

_____

_____

_____

5. Los Angeles is an important city.

It is not the capital of the United States.

_____

_____

_____

_____

_____

6. Coffee is delicious.

It is not really good for you.

_____

_____

_____

_____

7. The sky is often gray in the winter.

It is usually cold.

_____

_____

_____

_____

8. Cigarettes are bad.

_____

_____

_____

They are unhealthy.

_____

EXERCISE 4

**Why is your partner studying English? Why are you studying English?
Write two sentences that contain *because*.**

1. _____

   _____

2. _____

   _____

C *FOR EXAMPLE*

When the information in one sentence is an example of the generalization in
the sentence that comes before it, you can begin the second sentence with
the phrase *for example*. Here are some examples.

Generalization:

1. New York is the center
   of many activities.

Examples:

It is the financial and fashion
center of the country.

New York is the center of many
activities. For example, it is the
financial and fashion center of
the country.

Generalization:
_____

2. Trees are beautiful in every season.

Example:

In the autumn their red, orange, and yellow leaves are like a painting.

Trees are beautiful in every season. For example, in the autumn their red, orange, and yellow leaves are like a painting.

Fill in the blanks.

1. *For example* begins _____ .

2. There is a _____ after *for example*.

EXERCISE 5

Fill in the blanks to make a general statement. Use your own opinions. Then, write a sentence with *for example* that contains examples to support the general statement.

1. _____ is a _____ beach.

_____

_____

2. _____ are _____ animals.

_____

_____

EXERCISE 6

Punctuate each group of words to make one or two sentences. Remember to begin each sentence with a capital letter. Remember to

begin the names of people, cities, and countries with a capital letter. Remember to end each sentence with a period. Remember to use commas before *and* and *but*. Remember to use a comma after *for example*. The first few sentences are done for you.

1. the sky is gray and it is cold

   The sky is gray, and it is cold. _____

2. birds are good pets because their voices are beautiful

   Birds are good pets because their voices are beautiful. _____

3. my vacation is in the summer but it is not my favorite season

   My vacation is in the summer, but it is not my favorite season. _____

4. fruit is very colorful for example apples are red green and yellow

   Fruit is very colorful. For example, apples are red, green, and yellow. _____

5. washington and london are important because they are capitals

   _____

   _____

6. it is cool in the morning but it is warm in the afternoon

   _____

   _____

7. my classmates are from interesting countries for example two of them are from japan

   _____

   _____

8. vegetables are many different colors for example carrots are orange and spinach is green

   _____

   _____

   _____

9. linda is happy because it is warm today

_____

_____

10. ports are often important cities for example new york and boston are ports and they are important cities

_____

_____

6 GETTING READY TO WRITE A PARAGRAPH

Look at the sentences that you wrote in section 5, exercise 2. Choose one that you want to write about.

Tell your partner the sentence that you have chosen. Then, tell your partner why it is true. Let your partner ask you questions.

Now, write your sentence in the space provided.

_____

_____

_____

Now, make a list of other sentences that support your idea. Use the space provided.

Sentences That Support My Idea

_____

_____

_____

_____

_____

_____

_____

7 WRITING A PARAGRAPH

Review your work in section 4. Then, look at the list of sentences that you have just made. Do all of them support your first statement? Cross out any that do not.

Now, using a clean piece of paper, write a paragraph that supports your statement. Begin with the statement and follow it with the supporting sentences.

8 EXPANDING YOUR PARAGRAPH

Read your partner's paragraph. Let your partner read your paragraph.

Is there more information that you want from your partner? Write more questions for your partner to answer. Write them in your partner's book. Let your partner write questions in your book. Write answers to your partner's questions.

My Partner's Questions

_____

_____

_____

_____

_____

My Answers

_____

_____

_____

_____

_____

_____

9 REVISING AND EDITING

A REVISING

Read the answers that you wrote in section 8. Are they about the same topics as your paragraph? Do you want to add some of them to your paragraph?

Rewrite your paragraph on a clean piece of paper. Add the new information.

B EDITING

Read your partner's paragraph. Let your partner read your paragraph. Check your partner's paragraph for the following.

1. Do all of the sentences begin with a capital letter?
2. Do all of the sentences end with a period?
3. Are commas used correctly? (Review section 5.)
4. Do the names of people, cities, and countries begin with a capital letter?
5. Is the first sentence of the paragraph indented?
6. Are the pronoun forms correct? (Review section 3A.)
7. Are the noun forms correct? (Review section 3B.)

Give back your partner's paragraph. Look at your paragraph. Copy it again with any corrections that are necessary. Give your finished paragraph to your teacher.

10 MORE WRITING

Follow your teacher's instructions, or work on this section on your own if you have time.

1. Interview a classmate about his or her favorite season. Then, write a paragraph about that season and why it is his or her favorite.
2. What is your favorite food in the summer? Why?
3. What is your favorite animal? Why?

CHAPTER 3

Describing Countries and Other Places

Topic: Countries and other places

Rhetorical Focus: Adding details

Mechanical Focus: Periods and question marks; capitalizing place names

Grammatical Focus: *there is/there are*; prepositions; place names; direction words

Connectors and Transitions: Pronoun reference

1 PRE-WRITING: READING A MAP

Work with your partner. Discuss the map. Ask each other questions about it. Here are some ideas to get you started.

1. What country is this?
2. Is it a big country or a small country?
3. What oceans is it between?
4. What other countries is it between?
5. Are there any mountains? Where are they?
6. Where are the Great Plains?

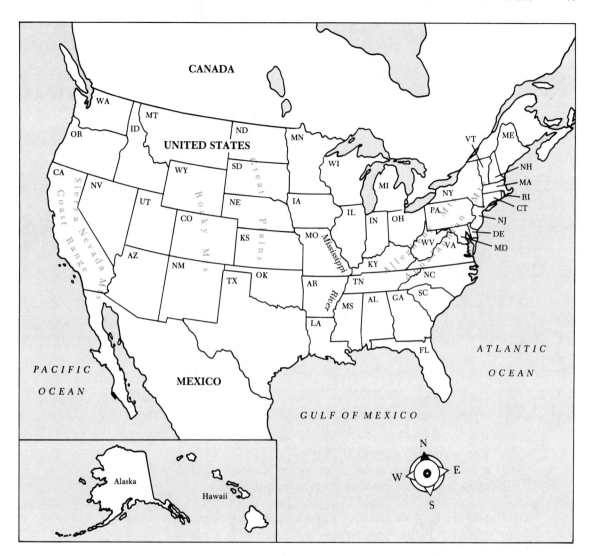

2 WRITING SENTENCES

A WRITING ABOUT A MAP OF THE UNITED STATES

After you discuss the map, write some questions about it in your partner's book. Ask your partner to write some questions in the space provided in your book. Begin each question with a capital letter and end it with a question mark.

My Partner's Questions

Here are some possible answers to the questions in section 1.

1. This is the United States.
2. It is a big country.
3. Most of it is between the Atlantic Ocean and the Pacific Ocean.
4. Most of it is between Canada and Mexico.
5. There are two mountain ranges. They are in the east and in the west.
6. The Great Plains are between the two mountain ranges.

Now, write answers to your partner's questions in the space provided. Use proper sentence form. Begin each sentence with a capital letter and end it with a period. Begin each important word in each proper noun with a capital letter.

Answers to My Partner's Questions

_____

_____

_____

_____

_____

_____

B   WRITING ABOUT A MAP OF ANOTHER COUNTRY

Bring a map of your country or another country that you would like
to visit to class. Show it to your partner. Let your partner write
questions about it in the space provided in your book. Write down
your answers to your partner's questions. Begin each sentence with a
capital letter. End each sentence with a period. Begin each important
word in every proper noun with a capital letter.

**My Partner's Questions
About My Map**

_____

_____

_____

_____

_____

_____

_____

_____

_____

My Answers to My Partner's
Questions About My Map

_____

_____

_____

_____

_____

_____

_____

_____

3 GRAMMAR

A REVIEW OF SIMPLE PRESENT FORMS OF THE VERB *TO BE*

EXERCISE 1

Fill in each blank with the correct simple present form of the verb *to be*.

1. The United States is a big country. It _____ in the western hemisphere.

2. The Great Plains are in the middle of the country. They _____ between two mountain ranges.

3. There are mountains in the east and in the west. Those in the east

_____ low and smooth. Those in the west _____ tall and rocky.

4. Canada and Mexico are in the western hemisphere. They _____

neighbors of the United States.

5. Canada is to the north of the United States. Mexico _____ to the south.

B USING *THERE* IN SENTENCES ABOUT LOCATION

> **Many English sentences about location begin with the word *there*.**
>
> 1. There are two big mountain ranges in the United States.
> 2. There is a big river between the two mountain ranges.

There is the grammatical subject of these sentences, but it is *neither singular nor plural*. The verb in sentences that begin with *there* agrees with the noun phrase that follows the verb. If the noun phrase is singular, the verb is singular. If the noun phrase is plural, the verb is plural.

there	*to be*	**Noun Phrase**	**Rest of the Sentence**
There	**is**	*a desert*	in the southwest.
There	**is**	*a big river*	in the east.
There	**are**	*three countries*	in North America.
There	**are**	*fifty states*	in the United States.

EXERCISE 2

Fill in each blank with the correct present form of the verb *to be*.

1. There are some questions in section 1. There _____ a map, too.

2. There are some maps in this chapter. There _____ a lot of questions and examples, too.

3. There are ten chapters in this book. There _____ pictures, photographs, or maps in each chapter.

4. The Great Plains are very fertile. There _____ many farms in this part of the country.

5. Forty-eight of the states in the United States _____ between the Atlantic Ocean and the Pacific Ocean.

6. There is a high mountain range in the west. There _____ a low one in the east.

EXERCISE 3

Look at the map of Australia. Fill in the blanks in the paragraph with the correct present form of the verb *to be*. Copy the paragraph correctly onto a clean piece of paper.

This _____ a map of Australia. It _____ a big country. It _____ in the Indian Ocean. Indonesia and Malaysia _____ to its north. The Tasman Sea _____ to its southeast. There _____ two big rivers in Australia. Both of them _____ in the east. There _____ a big desert in the west.

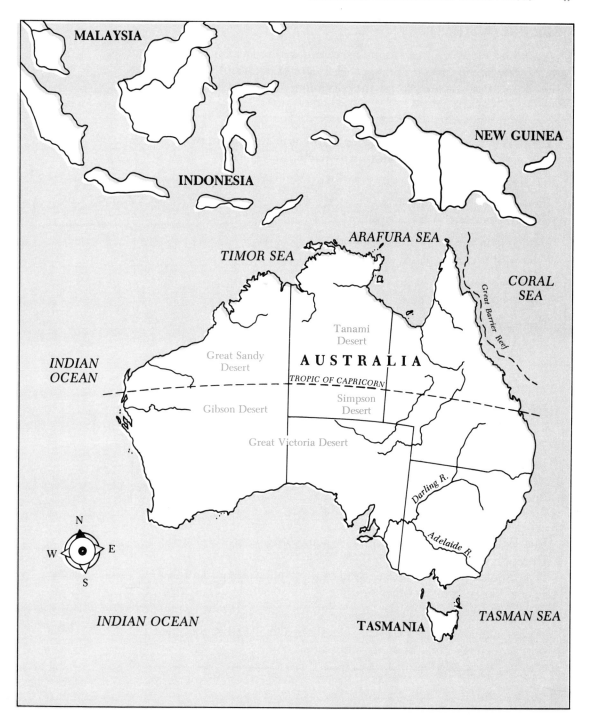

C PREPOSITIONS

Prepositions are words that can be used to describe location. In English, they occur *before nouns or noun phrases*. Here are examples of some common prepositions that are used to describe location.

IN   **When a place or object contains another place or object, the preposition *in* is used.**

Canada is in North America.
(North America contains Canada.)

Mexico is in the western hemisphere.
(The western hemisphere contains Mexico.)

There are deserts in some states.
(Some states contain deserts.)

There are farms in the Great Plains.
(The Great Plains contain farms.)

BETWEEN   **When something is on one side of a person, place, or object and something else is on the other side, the preposition *between* is used. For example, the number 4 is between 9 and 3.**

9   4   3

The United States is between the Atlantic Ocean and the Pacific Ocean.
(The Atlantic Ocean is on one side of the United States, and the Pacific Ocean is on its other side.)

The Great Plains are between two mountain ranges.
(One mountain range is on one side of the Great Plains, and the other mountain range is on its other side.)

> **TO**   When one place or object touches or nearly touches another one, the preposition *to* is used with a direction word to show where it touches or nearly touches.
>
> ---
>
> Canada is to the north of the United States.
> (Canada touches the northern part of the United States.)
>
> The Atlantic Ocean is to the east of Canada.
> (The Atlantic Ocean touches the eastern part of Canada.)

EXERCISE 4

Look at the map of England on the next page. Fill in the blanks in the following paragraph with one of the following prepositions. The first one is done for you.

in   between   to

This is a map of England. It is a small country ____*in*____

Europe. It is _____ the Atlantic Ocean.

St. George's Channel is _____ its southwest,

and the North Sea is _____ its northeast. The

English Channel is _____ England and France.

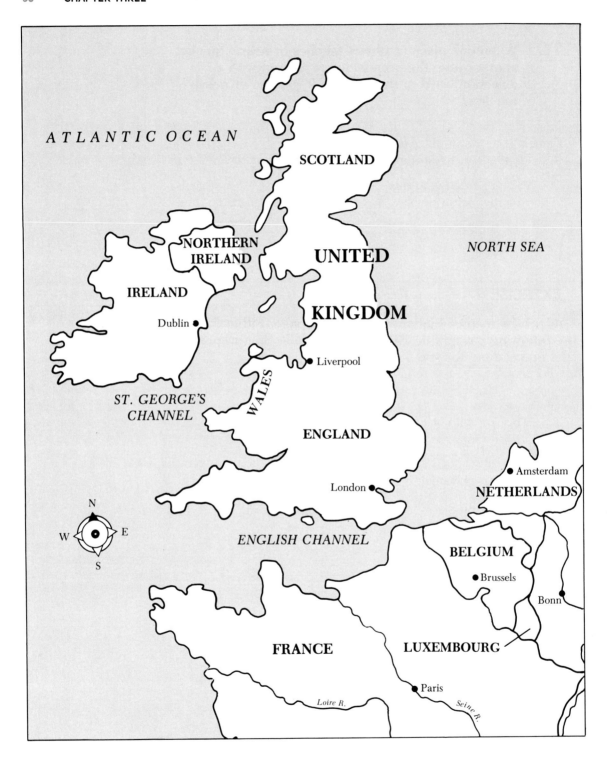

D PLACE NAMES

Place names are the *specific* names of places. Like the names of people, they are *proper nouns*.

Sentence with Common Noun	Sentence with Proper Noun
This is a map of *a country*. What *river* is that?	This is a map of **C**anada. It's the **M**ississippi **R**iver.

Because place names are proper nouns, all of the important words in them begin with a capital letter.

Many place names are made up of a common noun that is preceded by a specific name. In these cases, the place name begins with the article *the*. Here are some examples.

the	Specific Name	Common Noun
the	*Mississippi*	River
the	*Rocky*	Mountains
the	*Pacific*	Ocean

Not all proper nouns contain a specific name. Some of them are made up of an adjective followed by a common noun.

In most of these cases, *the* is also used at the beginning of the proper noun phrase. Here are some examples.

the	Adjective	Common Noun
the	*United*	States
the	*Great*	Plains
the	*North*	Sea

There are some exceptions to this rule. Most of them occur when the adjective is followed by a noun that is already a proper noun. Here are some examples.

Adjective	Proper Noun
New	**York**
(*York* is a city in England. It is a proper noun.)	
North	**America**
(*America* is the name of two continents. It is a proper noun.)	
Upper	**Volta**
(This is the old name of Burkina Faso, a country in Africa.)	
(*Volta* is a river. It is a proper noun.)	
New	**Mexico**
(*Mexico* is a country. It is a proper noun.)	

EXERCISE 5

Fill in each blank with a place name. Remember to use *the* when it is required and to begin all of the important words with a capital letter. The first two are done for you.

1. *Pacifico* means "calm" in Spanish. Sailors thought that that ocean was calm. That's why they called it ___the Pacific Ocean___.

2. People from England wanted to start a new city. They had connections with the city of York. That's why they called this new city ___New York___.

3. The mythical continent of Atlantis was supposed to be in the middle of this ocean. *Atlantic* is the adjective form of *Atlantis*. That's why the ocean is called _____ _____.

4. This continent is to the north of South America. That's why it's called _____ _____.

5. Those mountains are not very old. Therefore, they are quite rocky. That's why they are called _____.

6. Those plains are very big, or great. That's why they are called _____

_____.

E DIRECTION WORDS

Look at the map of the United States in section 1. Look at the compass in the lower right corner. It shows the different geographic directions. These directions have noun and adjective forms.

Noun	Adjective
north	northern
south	southern
east	eastern
west	western
northeast	northeastern
northwest	northwestern
southeast	southeastern
southwest	southwestern

EXERCISE 6

Use the map in section 1 to help you fill in the blanks in the following sentences. Be sure to use the correct form of the direction word. The first two are done for you.

1. Florida is in the ___southeastern___ United States.

2. California is to the ___south___ of Oregon.

3. New York is in the _____ United States.

4. Georgia is to the _____ of Florida.

5. Texas is to the _____ of Louisiana.

6. North Dakota is in the _____ United States.

EXERCISE 7

Choose one of the other maps in this chapter and write three questions about that map for your partner. Use direction words in your questions. Here is an example of a question about the map of the United States.

What state is to the north of Oregon?

Write the questions in your partner's book. Let your partner write questions in your book.

My Partner's Questions About
the Map of _____

_____

_____

_____

_____

_____

_____

_____

_____

_____

_____

_____

_____

_____

Now, answer your partner's questions. Use complete sentences.

My Answers to My Partner's Questions
About the Map of _____

_____

_____

_____

_____

_____

_____

_____

_____

_____

_____

_____

4 EDITING

Look at the sentences that your partner wrote in section 2 to answer your questions. Check them for the following:

1. Does each sentence begin with a capital letter?
2. Does each sentence end with a period?
3. Does each important word in every proper noun begin with a capital letter?
4. Are the place names correct? (Review section 3D.)
5. Are the prepositions correct? (Review section 3C.)
6. Are the geographic direction words correct? (Review section 3E.)

Correct your partner's sentences and ask your partner to correct your sentences.

After your partner corrects your sentences, copy them onto a clean sheet of paper and give them to your teacher.

5 CONNECTORS AND TRANSITIONS

THIRD-PERSON PRONOUNS AND POSSESSIVE ADJECTIVES

In English, the correct form of a pronoun or possessive adjective depends on whether the antecedent noun or noun phrase is singular or plural. It also depends on the function of the pronoun or possessive adjective in the sentence.

In Chapter 1, you studied subject pronouns and possessive adjectives. Now, you are going to review their third-person forms and learn the third-person object forms.

Antecedent	Subject Pronoun	Rest of the Sentence
This is a map of the *United States.*	**It**	is a big country. (Remember: Because *the United States* is the name of *one* country, it is *singular.*)
Canada and the United States are big countries.	**They**	are in the western hemisphere.

Antecedent	Possessive Adjective	
Australia is in the Indian Ocean.	The Tasman Sea is to **its**	southeast.
Canada, the United States, and Mexico are in North America.	The Atlantic Ocean is to **their**	east.

Antecedent		Preposition Plus Object Pronoun
The United States is between two other countries.	Canada is to the north	of **it.**
Canada and Mexico are in the western hemisphere.	The United States is	between **them.**

Fill in the blanks.

1. An _____ pronoun comes after a preposition.

2. The third-person object pronouns are _____ and _____.

EXERCISE 1

Read the paragraphs about Australia, England, and the United States. (You completed the first two in section 3.) Begin this exercise by underlining all examples of *it, its, they, them,* and *their.*

Then, draw a circle around each antecedent. Draw an arrow from the underlined pronoun or possessive adjective to its antecedent. The first paragraph is done for you.

1. (Look at the map on page 47.)

Australia

This is the map of Australia. It is a big country. It is in the

Indian Ocean. Indonesia and Malaysia are to its north. The

Tasman Sea is to its southeast. There are two big rivers in

Australia. Both of them are in the east. There is a big desert

in the west.

2. (Look at the map on page 50.)

England

This is a map of England. It is a small country in Europe.

It is in the Atlantic Ocean. St. George's Channel is to its

southwest, and the North Sea is to its northeast. The English

Channel is between England and France.

3. (Look at the map on page 41.)

The United States

This is a map of the United States. It is a big country.

Most of it is between the Atlantic Ocean and the Pacific

Ocean. Most of it is between Canada and Mexico. There are

two mountain ranges. They are in the east and in the west.

The Great Plains are between the two mountain ranges.

EXERCISE 2

**Fill in each blank with one of the following: *it, its, they, them,* or
their. Then, draw a circle around the antecedent. Draw an arrow
connecting the word you wrote to the antecedent.**

1. Mexico is in North America. _____ is to the south of the

   United States.

2. The Great Plains are in the middle of the United States. _____

are very fertile.

3. There are two big mountain ranges in the United States. The Great

   Plains are between _____.

4. The United States is a country in North America. _____ capital

   is Washington, D.C.

5. Canada and Mexico are in the western hemisphere. The United States

   is _____ neighbor.

6. Australia is a continent and a country. _____ is in the Indian

   Ocean.

6 GETTING READY TO WRITE A PARAGRAPH

SPATIAL ORDER

We use spatial order when we write a paragraph that focuses on locations. We usually begin a spatially organized paragraph by telling the reader what the *topic* of the paragraph will be. Reread the paragraph about the United States on page 58.

What is the first sentence?

_____

_____

What does it tell the reader?

_____

_____

Next, we make a *comment* about the topic of the paragraph. A comment tells more about the topic.

What is the second sentence in the paragraph about the United States?

_____

_____

Does it contain a topic or a comment?

_____

_____

After this short introduction, we can begin to tell the reader about the location of our topic.

What are the third and fourth sentences in the paragraph about the United States?

_____

_____

_____

_____

What are they about?

_____

_____

Finally, we may tell the reader about the locations of things *inside* our topic.

What are the last three sentences in the paragraph about the United States?

_____

_____

_____

_____

_____

_____

What are they about?

_____

_____

_____

_____

EXERCISE

Read the sentences that can be used to write a paragraph about the map of Canada on the next page. Work with your partner to put them into proper order to make a spatially organized paragraph. Use (1) for the first sentence, (2) for the second, and so on. Then, copy the sentences in proper paragraph form onto a clean sheet of paper. Give the paragraph to your teacher.

_____ The Mackenzie River is in the west.

_____ It is to the north of the United States.

_____ This is a map of Canada.

_____ There aren't any big cities near it.

_____ Ottawa is the capital of Canada.

_____ It is a big country.

_____ It is near the St. Lawrence River.

_____ It is between the Atlantic and the Pacific Oceans.

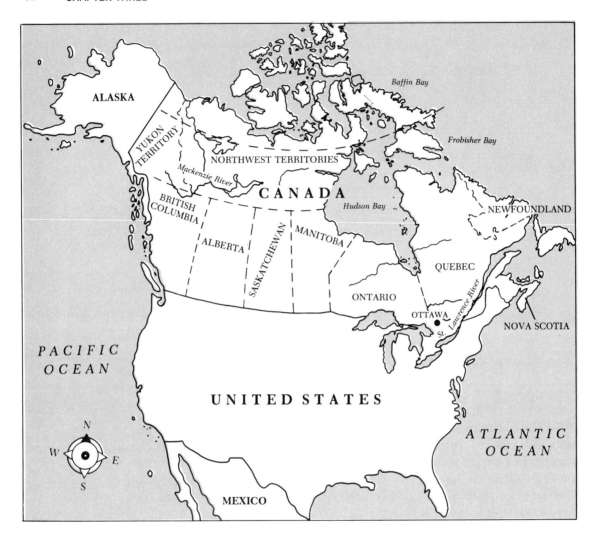

7 WRITING A PARAGRAPH

Reread the sentences that you wrote to answer your partner's
questions about your map in section 2B. Write a paragraph about the
country on a clean piece of paper. Use proper paragraph form.
Indent the first sentence.

8 EXPANDING YOUR PARAGRAPH

A GEOGRAPHIC DETAILS

Geographic details about a country give information about the location of the country or about the locations of places in it.

Reread the paragraph about the map of the United States on page 58. Can you and your partner find four sentences that contain geographic details? What are they?

Geographic Details
About the United States

1. _____

   _____

2. _____

   _____

3. _____

   _____

4. _____

   _____

Now, reread the paragraph that you wrote about a country in section 7. It probably contains at least three geographic details. Copy the sentences that describe these details.

Geographic Details
About _____

_____

_____

_____

_____

_____

_____

_____

_____

B ADDING INFORMATION

These details mention specific places. Here are two specific places from the paragraph about the United States.

> two mountain ranges
> the Great Plains

Choose two specific places that you mention in your paragraph. Write the names of each of the places at the top of a piece of paper. Give the paper to your partner. Ask your partner to write questions about each of the places. After your partner returns the paper, write answers to the questions. If you are not sure of some of the answers, you can go to the library or ask your teacher to recommend a book to look in.

Here are some questions and answers about the two places mentioned in the paragraph about the United States.

two mountain ranges
Can you describe the mountain ranges?
The mountains in the east are low and smooth. The mountains in the west are high and rocky. This is because the mountains in the east are old, and the mountains in the west are not very old.

the Great Plains	
What kind of land are they?	
	The Great Plains are very fertile.
What can you find there?	
	There are many farms in the Great Plains. Two very important crops are wheat and corn.

C WRITING PARAGRAPHS THAT CONTAIN ADDED INFORMATION

In this section, you are going to write several paragraphs. Use a clean piece of paper for each one. Use proper paragraph form. (Review page 15.)

Now, you can use your answers from section 8B to write a paragraph about each of the specific places.

Here are two paragraphs about the two mountain ranges and the Great Plains in the United States.

> **There are mountains** in the eastern and western parts of the United States. The mountains **in the east** are low and smooth because they are old. Those **in the west** are very tall and rocky because they are not very old.
> **The Great Plains are** a large part of the land **between the eastern and western mountains**. This part is very fertile. There are many farms in the Great Plains. Two very important crops are wheat and corn.

Now, try to expand the first sentences in your paragraph. Give some more information about the location of your country. You may use some other information from your paragraph.

Here is an expanded paragraph based on the first sentences of the paragraph about the United States. The information from the original paragraph is highlighted.

> **This is a map of the United States. It is a big country** in the western hemisphere. Most of it is in North America. **It is between** two oceans. **The Atlantic Ocean** is to its east, **and the Pacific Ocean** is to its west. **It is** also **between** two other countries. **Canada** is to its north, **and Mexico** is to its south.

You now have the first three paragraphs of an essay about your country. Here is what they look like for an essay based on the paragraph about the United States.

> This is a map of the United States. It is a big country in the western hemisphere. Most of it is in North America. It is between two oceans. The Atlantic Ocean is to its east, and the Pacific Ocean is to its west. It is also between two other countries. Canada is to its north, and Mexico is to its south.
>
> There are mountains in the eastern and western parts of the United States. The mountains in the east are low and smooth because they are old. Those in the west are very tall and rocky because they are not very old.
>
> The Great Plains are a large part of the land between the eastern and western mountains. This part is very fertile. There are many farms in the Great Plains. Two very important crops are wheat and corn.

D WRITING A CONCLUSION

All that you need now is a conclusion, or final paragraph. Discuss your three paragraphs with your partner. What idea seems very important when you talk about them?

Two of the paragraphs about the United States discuss the different types of land, so the following idea seems very important.

> The United States is a big country with a varied topography.

Now, discuss the important idea from your paragraphs with your partner. What can you say to expand it? Write some sentences.

Here are some expansions of the idea from the paragraphs about the United States.

> The land is different.
> There are farms and cities.
> The scenery is different.
> The people are different.
> There are many rivers and lakes, too.

Choose two or three of your expansions to add to your sentence. Add information to them if you want to. Then, combine your original sentence and your expansions to make a conclusion to your essay.

Here is the conclusion for the essay about the United States.

> The United States is a big country with a varied topography. The scenery is quite different in different parts of the country. Like the scenery, the people are quite different in different sections, too.

Here is what a four-paragraph essay about the United States looks like. The information that was in the original paragraph is highlighted.

> **This is a map of the United States. It is a big country** in the western hemisphere. Most of it is in North America. **It is between** two oceans. **The Atlantic Ocean** is to its east, **and the Pacific Ocean** is to its west. **It is** also **between** two other countries. **Canada** is to its north, **and Mexico** is to its south.
> **There are mountains** in the eastern and western parts of the United States. The mountains **in the east** are low and smooth because they are old. Those **in the west** are very tall and rocky because they are not very old.
> **The Great Plains are** a large part of the land **between the eastern and western mountains.** This part is very fertile. There are many farms in the Great Plains. Two very important crops are wheat and corn.
> The United States is a big country with a varied topography. The scenery is quite different in different parts of the country. Like the scenery, the people are quite different in different sections, too.

Now, on a clean piece of paper, write the first draft of an essay about your country.

9 REVISING AND EDITING

A REVISING

Read your partner's essay, and let your partner read your essay.
1. Are there paragraphs about specific parts of the country? Is each of these paragraphs about only one part?
2. Is there a conclusion?
3. Do you want your partner to add any information?

Write a second draft of your essay.

B EDITING

Read your partner's second draft, and let your partner read your second draft.

1. Are the paragraphs in correct paragraph form?
2. Does each sentence begin with a capital letter?
3. Does each sentence end with a period?
4. Does each important word in every proper noun begin with a capital letter?
5. Are the place names correct? (Review section 3D.)
6. Are the prepositions correct? (Review section 3C.)
7. Are the geographic direction words correct? (Review section 3E.)

Write a third draft of your essay on a clean piece of paper, and give it to your teacher.

10 MORE WRITING

Follow your teacher's instructions, or work on this section on your own if you have time.

1. Draw a plan of your bedroom or another room at home. Show it to your partner. Let your partner ask you questions about it. Write answers to your partner's questions.

   Choose some of your answers to make a spatially organized paragraph about your room. Write your paragraph on another piece of paper. Use proper paragraph form.

Then, let another classmate read your paragraph. Ask that classmate to draw a picture of your room based on your paragraph. Does the drawing look like your room? What changes can you make in your paragraph to make the information clearer?

2. Discuss your essay about your country with your partner. What additional information can you add? Let your partner ask you more questions about it. Write answers to your partner's questions about your essay. Choose some of the answers to add to your essay.

Here is an expansion of the essay about the United States.

The United States is a big country in the western hemisphere. Most of it is on the continent of North America. It is between two oceans. The Atlantic Ocean is on its east coast, and the Pacific Ocean is on its west coast. It is also between two other countries. Canada is to its north, and Mexico is to its south.

The eastern and western parts of the United States are very different from each other. There are mountains in both parts, but the mountains in the east are low and smooth because they are old. Those in the west are very tall and rocky because they are not very old. The land in the east is very fertile. There are a lot of trees and grass. There are some trees and grass in the west, but there are also deserts in some states.

The Great Plains are a large part of the land between the eastern and western mountains. This part is also very fertile. There are many farms there. Two very important crops are wheat and corn.

The climate is also very different in different sections of the United States. There are two seasons in almost all parts, but the characteristics of each season are different. For example, winter in the southern states is usually mild. The amount of rain is also very different. For instance, the southwest is very dry, and the northwest very humid.

The United States is a big country with a varied topography and climate. The scenery is quite different from one part to another. Like the scenery, the people are quite different in different sections, too.

CHAPTER 4

Describing People and What They Are Doing

Topic: Classmates and other people

Rhetorical Focus: Supporting ideas

Mechanical Focus: Using commas before *too* and *either*

Grammatical Focus: The present continuous tense; objects; pronouns and possessive adjectives; phrasal prepositions; prepositional phrases

Connectors and Transitions: *too* and *either*; using prepositional phrases to connect sentences and paragraphs

1 PRE-WRITING: CHOOSING THE GENERAL IDEA

Look at the pictures. Discuss them with your partner. Circle the adjective or phrase that best describes the person or people in each picture. Circle the verbs that describe what the person is doing. The first one is done for you.

A

happy   crying

sick   closing his eyes

tired   reading

                      resting

B

angry	arguing
happy	laughing
sick	crying
	frowning
	shouting

C

good athletes	playing baseball
bad students	studying
good students	doing homework
	watching TV

You were able to choose the best adjective or phrase to describe each person or each group of people because you saw the picture. The actions in the pictures helped you to get a *general idea* of the situation. They *support* or *prove* the *general idea.*

D

angry	eating ice cream
happy	smiling
sad	sleeping
	yawning

2 WRITING SENTENCES

Write sentences about the pictures on pages 70 and 71. Use the words that you circled in your sentences.

Picture (A)

_____

_____

_____

_____

_____

Picture (B)

_____

_____

_____

_____

_____

Picture (C)

_____

_____

_____

_____

_____

Picture (D)

_____

_____

_____

3 GRAMMAR

A THE PRESENT CONTINUOUS TENSE

> **We use the present continuous tense to describe what is happening now or what is happening in a photograph or picture.**
>
> I **am reading** my English book.
> You **are reading** your English book, too.
> That man **is closing** his eyes.
> That woman **is smiling**.
> It **isn't raining**.
> They **are arguing**. They **aren't laughing**.

Fill in the blanks.

1. The present continuous tense has _____ parts.

2. The first part is the simple present form of the verb _____ .

3. The second part is a verb that ends in -_____ .

> **The -*ing* form of the verb is formed by adding -*ing* to the base form of the verb.**
>
> | Base Form | -*ing* Form |
> |-----------|-------------|
> | cry | cry**ing** |
> | frown | frown**ing** |
> | laugh | laugh**ing** |
> | shout | shout**ing** |
> | yawn | yawn**ing** |
> | talk | talk**ing** |

Most verbs that end in the letter *e* drop the *e* when they add *-ing*.	
Base Form with *e*	***-ing* Form Without *e***
argue	arguing
close	closing
smile	smiling

One-syllable verbs that contain one vowel and end in one consonant double the consonant when they add *-ing*.	
One-Syllable Base Form with One Vowel Ending in One Consonant	***-ing* Form with Double Consonant**
rub	rubbing
sit	sitting

One-syllable verbs that contain two vowels and end in one consonant do not double the consonant when they add *-ing*.	
One-Syllable Base Form with Two Vowels Ending in One Consonant	***-ing* Form with Single Consonant**
eat	eating
look	looking
read	reading
wear	wearing

One-syllable verbs that end in more than one consonant do not double any consonants when they add *-ing*.	
One-Syllable Base Form Ending in Two Consonants	***-ing* Form Without Doubling**
ta**lk**	ta**lking**
lau**gh**	lau**ghing**

EXERCISE 1

The following paragraphs are about the picture of the basketball game. Ask your partner or your teacher about the meaning of any words that you do not understand.

The base form of each verb is given in parentheses next to a blank. Fill in the correct form of the present continuous tense in each blank.

The first one is done for you. Then, copy the paragraphs onto a clean piece of paper. Give the paper to your teacher.

This is a picture of an exciting basketball game. The fans are very excited. They _____*are watching*_____ (watch) the game. They _____ (root) for their team. Some of them _____ (shout). Some of them _____ (smile).

The players are excited, too. Some of them _____ _____ (run). One of them _____ (hold) the ball. He is near the basket. Two other players _____ (block) him.

B OBJECTS

In Chapter 3, you learned that the word that comes after a preposition is called an *object*.

Read the following sentences in which the objects are underlined.

1. The fans are watching the game.
2. They are rooting for their team.
3. One of the players is holding the ball.

Then fill in the blanks.

1. An object can occur after a preposition or a _____ .

2. A pronoun or noun phrase that occurs after a preposition or after a verb

   (except the verb *to be*) is called an _____ .

EXERCISE 2

Underline the object in each sentence. The first one is done for you.

1. I'm sitting in my classroom. My teacher is looking at me.

2. You are doing your homework. Your brother is helping you.

3. A player is holding the ball. Two other players are blocking him.

4. The woman is eating ice cream. Her friend is standing next to her.

5. The fans are watching the basketball game. They are enjoying it.

6. We are watching television. Our friends are sitting with us.

7. You are sitting near us, and we are sitting near you.

8. The players are running to the basket. The fans are rooting for them.

C PRONOUNS AND POSSESSIVE ADJECTIVES

Subject Pronoun	Object Pronoun	Possessive Adjective
I	me	my
you	you	your
he	him	his
she	her	her
it	it	its
we	us	our
you	you	your
they	them	their

EXERCISE 3

Fill in each blank with a correct pronoun or possessive adjective. The first one is done for you.

1. Our teacher is standing near _____ us _____ .

2. My eyes are blue, and _____ hair is brown.

3. The book is open. Linda is reading _____ .

4. The man is shouting. The other people are looking at _____ .

5. The students are closing _____ eyes.

6. We are in Linda's class, and you are in _____ , too.

7. The players are running. The fans are watching _____ .

8. I am sitting next to Karen, and she is sitting next to _____ .

D PHRASAL PREPOSITIONS THAT SHOW LOCATION

Paolo is a student in Linda's class. Look at the picture of her class, then read the sentences that Paolo wrote.

1. There is a student from Japan in front of me.
2. There is a student from Greece next to him.
3. There is a student from Lebanon in back of her.

Fill in the blanks.

1. *In front of*, *in back of*, and *next to* are called phrasal prepositions. A

   phrasal preposition contains _____ or _____ words.

2. A phrasal preposition functions like a _____ .

EXERCISE 4

Now, write three sentences about where the students in your class are sitting. (You may use their names.) Use the phrasal prepositions *in front of, in back of,* and *next to.*

1. _____

_____

2. _____

_____

3. _____

_____

E   USING PREPOSITIONAL PHRASES AS MODIFIERS

Read these sentences about the woman in picture (D) in section 1.

1. There is a woman next to the tree.
2. Her hair is black.

These can be combined into one sentence that contains a prepositional phrase that modifies *a woman.*

There is a woman *with black hair* next to the tree.

Fill in the blanks.

1. A prepositional phrase consists of a preposition followed by a

_____ and any modifiers or a pronoun.

2. The first word in a prepositional phrase is a _____ .

3. The last word in a prepositional phrase is a _____ or a pronoun.

Combine each pair of sentences to make one sentence that contains a prepositional phrase that modifies one of the nouns. Then, answer the questions after the exercise. The first one is done for you.

1. There is a player near the basket.

   He is wearing white shorts.

   There is a player in white shorts near the basket.

2. There is a man under the clock.

   His hair is black.

   _____

   _____

   _____

   _____

3. There are two people in the parking lot.

   Their faces are angry.

   _____

   _____

   _____

   _____

   (Use the preposition *with*.)

4. There is a woman under the tree.

   She is wearing blue pants.

   _____

   _____

   _____

   _____

5. There is a student in front
   of me.

   _____

   _____

   _____

   He is from Japan.   _____

What preposition is used for body parts? _____

What preposition is used for clothing? _____

What preposition is used for place of origin? _____

4 EDITING

Show your partner the sentences that you wrote in section 2 of this chapter. Look at your partner's sentences.

1. Are the present forms of the verb *to be* correct?
2. Are the *-ing* forms of the verbs correct? (Review section 3A.)
3. Are the object pronouns correct? (Review section 3C.)
4. Are the phrasal prepositions correct? (Review section 3D.)
5. Are the prepositional phrases used as modifiers correct? (Review section 3E.)
6. Does each sentence begin with a capital letter?
7. Does each name begin with a capital letter?

Correct your partner's sentences, and ask your partner to correct your sentences. Copy the corrected sentences onto a clean sheet of paper and give them to your teacher.

5 CONNECTORS AND TRANSITIONS

A *TOO* AND *EITHER*

TOO When two affirmative sentences share a subject, verb, or adjective, *too* is often used at the end of the second sentence.

Shared Subject:
The man is yawning. **He** is closing his eyes, **too**.
(Note that a pronoun is used for the subject of the second sentence.)

Shared Verb:
The students **are laughing**. The teacher **is (laughing)**, **too**.
(Note that the shared *-ing* form of the verb can be left out in the second sentence.)

Shared Adjective:
The fans are **excited**. The players are **(excited), too**.
(Note that the shared adjective can be left out in the second sentence.)

EITHER When two negative sentences share a subject, verb, or adjective, *either* is often used at the end of the second sentence.

Shared Subject:
Linda isn't laughing. **She** isn't smiling, **either**.

Shared Verb:
The fans **aren't laughing**. The players **aren't (laughing)**, **either**.

Shared Adjective:
Linda isn't **tired**. James isn't **(tired)**, **either**.

Answer the question in the space provided.

What punctuation mark comes before *too* and *either*? _____

EXERCISE 1

Complete the second sentence in each pair. Use *too* or *either*. The first two are done for you.

1. The players are shouting. The fans ___*are shouting, too*___.

2. The students aren't reading. They ___*aren't writing, either*___.

3. Ping is reading a book. Linda _____

   _____

4. It isn't snowing. _____ raining _____

5. Linda's class is studying English. Mary's class _____

   _____

6. Our class isn't taking a test. Their class _____

   _____

7. The tea isn't hot. _____ cold _____

8. I am reading. _____ writing _____

9. It's warm. _____ sunny _____

B OBJECT PRONOUNS AND ANTECEDENTS

EXERCISE 2

Read Paolo's paragraph on the next page about the students in Linda's class. The object pronouns are underlined. Draw a circle around each antecedent. Then, draw an arrow from the object pronoun to its antecedent.

I am sitting in my classroom and looking at the other

students. There is a student from Japan in front of <u>me</u>. There

is a student from Greece next to <u>him</u>. There is a student

from Lebanon behind <u>her</u>.

C USING PREPOSITIONAL PHRASES AS CONNECTORS

The prepositional phrases help to connect the sentences in the paragraph in exercise 2 in this section with each other. If the prepositional phrase comes at the beginning of a sentence, it is closer to its antecedent. This can make the sentences in a paragraph more connected.

Here is how the paragraph in exercise 2 in this section can be rewritten with prepositional phrases at the beginnings of the sentences.

I am sitting in my classroom and looking at the other students. In front of me, there is a student from Japan. Next to him, there is a student from Greece. Behind her, there is a student from Lebanon.

Answer the question in the space provided.

When a prepositional phrase begins a sentence, what punctuation mark

comes after it? _____

EXERCISE 3

Rewrite the sentences that you wrote about your classmates in exercise 4 in section 3D. Begin each of your sentences with a prepositional phrase.

6 GETTING READY TO WRITE A PARAGRAPH

THE MAIN IDEA AND SUPPORTING IDEAS

Every paragraph is about something. It has a topic and it makes a comment about that topic. What the paragraph is about is called the *main idea.*

Most paragraphs contain other information that *supports* the main idea. This information is called *supporting* details.

Read this short paragraph based on picture A in section 1.

> Kevin is resting. He is closing his eyes, too. It is two o'clock in the afternoon, but he is tired.

Discuss the paragraph with your partner. Choose the correct answer for each of the following questions.

1. What is the main idea of the paragraph?
   a. Kevin is closing his eyes.
   b. It is two o'clock in the afternoon.
   c. Kevin is tired.
   d. Kevin is resting.
2. Circle the sentences that support the main idea.
   a. It is two o'clock in the afternoon.
   b. Kevin is tired.
   c. Kevin is closing his eyes.
   d. Kevin is resting.

Answer these questions.

1. In the first paragraph about the basketball game on page 76, the second sentence expresses the main idea. What is this sentence?

   _____

2. What three sentences support the main idea?

   a. _____

   b. _____

   c. _____

7 WRITING A PARAGRAPH

EXERCISE 1

Work with your partner. Choose a picture from section 1. Look at the
sentences that you wrote about that picture in section 2. Discuss the
picture. On a clean piece of paper, write a short paragraph about it.
Remember to write a sentence that contains a main or general idea.
Remember to support your general idea with details.

EXERCISE 2

Complete this paragraph about people in your class. Use
prepositional phrases to modify or describe the people. Choose the
word or phrase in parentheses that describes where people are.

    I am sitting in my classroom and looking at the other

students. (Next to, In front of, In back of, Close to) _____

_____ me, there is a student _____

_____ . (Next to, In front of, In back of, Close to) _____

_____ (him, her) _____, there is a

student _____. (Behind, Next to, In front

of, Near) _____ this student, there is a

student _____ . There are (eight, ten,

fifteen, twenty, . . .) _____ students in

my class.

8 EXPANDING YOUR PARAGRAPH

A FREEWRITING

The paragraph that you completed in section 7 tells where the people
in your class are, but it does not really express a general idea about

them. Discuss the people in your class with your partner. Are there any general statements that you can make about all of them, most of them, or some of them? For example, are they from the same country or the same part of the world? Are they good students? Are they tired? Are all of them writing?

After you discuss your classmates with your partner, use the space provided to write down any general ideas that you have. Write for five minutes. Don't worry about whether your statements are correct or logical. Just keep writing. Don't lift your pen or pencil from your paper. If you can't think of anything to write, write your name or another word. Don't go back. Don't cross out anything.

General Ideas About My Classmates

_____

_____

_____

_____

_____

_____

_____

_____

_____

_____

_____

_____

_____

_____

_____

Look at the picture of Linda's English class on page 78. Here is some of Paolo's freewriting about the class.

General Ideas About the Students
in Linda's Class

not writing   sitting in their chairs
from many countries   young people
yawning   college students
tired this morning   rubbing their eyes

B CHOOSING A GENERAL IDEA TO WRITE ABOUT

Show your partner the list of ideas that you wrote while freewriting about your classmates. Look at your partner's list. Talk about what you wrote. Try to find ideas that go together. Draw lines around the ideas that go together.

Here is how Paolo grouped his ideas.

not writing   sitting in their chairs
from many countries   young people
yawning   college students
tired this morning   rubbing their eyes

After you group your ideas, choose one idea or group of ideas that you want to write about. Here is the group that Paolo chose.

yawning
tired this morning
rubbing their eyes

C FINDING DETAILS TO SUPPORT YOUR GENERAL IDEA

Discuss your idea or group of ideas with your partner.

1. If you chose a group, is one of them more general than the others?
2. Can you find other ideas that support your general idea?

Spend ten minutes freewriting about details about the students in your class that support your general idea. Follow the instructions for freewriting on pages 86 and 87.

Details That Support My General
Idea About My Classmates

My General Idea: _____

Supporting Ideas: _____

_____

_____

_____

_____

_____

_____

_____

_____

_____

_____

_____

_____

_____

_____

_____

_____

_____

_____

Here are some details that Paolo added.

My General Idea: *My class is tired this morning.*

Supporting Ideas:

The student from Greece is yawning.

My hair is messy.

face not shaved

The student from Lebanon

yawning

rubbing his eyes

The student from Japan is rubbing his eyes.

trying to write

having trouble

D   LOCATING THE STUDENTS THAT YOU WANT TO WRITE ABOUT

Look at the paragraph about your classmates that you completed in section 7, exercise 2. Does it include all of the students that you want to write about? Does it include any other students? Rewrite the paragraph so that it includes only the students that you want to write about.

E   THE PARTS OF A SHORT ESSAY

An essay is a group of paragraphs on the same subject. A short essay may contain an *introductory paragraph*, a *body*, and a *conclusion*.

F   WRITING A SHORT INTRODUCTORY PARAGRAPH

An introductory paragraph for a short essay tells what you are writing about and what your general idea is.

Here is Paolo's introductory paragraph.

I am sitting in my classroom and looking at the other students. Most of the students in my class are tired.

Copy the first sentence of the paragraph that you wrote in section 8D. Then, add one more sentence that states your general idea.

<u>**My Introductory Paragraph About My Classmates**</u>

_____

_____

_____

_____

_____

_____

G   WRITING THE BODY OF A SHORT ESSAY

The *body* of an essay is the name for the paragraphs after the introduction and before the conclusion. It contains information that *supports the main idea* of the essay.

Here is most of the body of Paolo's essay.

In front of me, there is a student from Japan. He is sleepy, too. He is trying to write, but he is having trouble. He is rubbing his eyes.

Next to him, there is a student from Greece. She isn't writing anything, either. Her pen is on her paper. She is yawning.

In back of her, there is a student from Lebanon. He is yawning, too. He is rubbing his eyes. He is sleepy.

Begin the body of your short essay by copying each of your sentences about one of your classmates. Then, look at the details that you wrote in freewriting in section 8C. Write sentences containing these details after each sentence about one of your classmates. While you are writing, you may think of more details. Add these details to your paragraph.

Paragraphs for the Body of My Short Essay

_____

_____

_____

_____

_____

_____

_____

_____

_____

_____

_____

_____

_____

_____

_____

_____

_____

_____

_____

_____

_____

_____

_____

_____

_____

_____

_____

_____

_____

_____

Here is the paragraph that Paolo wrote about himself. It is also part of the body of his short essay.

My hair is messy, and my face isn't shaved. I am sleepy.

If you wrote details about yourself in your freewriting, expand them into another paragraph for the body of your short essay.

My Paragraph About Myself

_____

_____

_____

_____

_____

_____

_____

_____

_____

H WRITING A CONCLUSION FOR A SHORT ESSAY

In a short essay, the last paragraph is the *conclusion*.

Here is what Paolo wrote for a concluding paragraph.

> There are twelve students in my class. Most of them are tired, including me.

You can write a conclusion by copying the last sentence of the paragraph that you wrote in section 8D. Then, add a sentence that restates your general idea. Try to use words that are different from the ones you used in your introductory paragraph.

My Concluding Paragraph About My Class

_____

_____

_____

_____

_____

_____

_____

I PUTTING PARAGRAPHS TOGETHER TO MAKE A SHORT ESSAY

You can combine your paragraphs to make a short essay. Here is the short essay that Paolo wrote.

> I am sitting in my classroom and looking at the other students. Most of the students in my class are tired.
> My hair is messy, and my face isn't shaved. I am sleepy.
> In front of me, there is a student from Japan. He is sleepy, too. He is trying to write, but he is having trouble. He is rubbing his eyes.

Next to him, there is a student from Greece. She isn't writing anything, either. Her pen is on her paper. She is yawning.

In back of her, there is a student from Lebanon. He is yawning, too. He is rubbing his eyes. He is sleepy.

There are twelve students in my class. Most of them are tired, including me.

Write a first draft of your short essay about your classmates on a clean piece of paper. Begin with the introductory paragraph. Then, write the paragraphs that are the body of your essay. (Begin the body with your paragraph about yourself if you wrote one.) Then, finish your essay with the conclusion.

9 REVISING AND EDITING

A REVISING

Read the first draft of your partner's short essay. Let your partner read the first draft of your essay. Let your partner make suggestions about the content of your essay. Make suggestions about the content of your partner's essay.

1. Does the introductory paragraph contain the main idea?
2. Does the concluding paragraph state the main idea in a different way?
3. Is each paragraph in the body of the essay about a different student?
4. Does each paragraph in the body contain details that support the main idea?
5. Are there any sentences that do not belong in the essay?
6. Can you suggest any other details that your partner can add?

Use your partner's suggestions to help you revise your essay. Then, write the second draft on a clean piece of paper.

B EDITING

Proofread the second draft of your partner's essay, and ask your partner to proofread your second draft.

1. Are the present forms of the verb *to be* correct?
2. Are the *-ing* forms of the verbs correct? (Review section 3A.)
3. Are the object pronouns correct? (Review section 3C.)

4. Are the phrasal prepositions correct? (Review section 3D.)
5. Are the prepositional phrases used as modifiers correct? (Review section 3E.)
6. Are *too* and *either* used correctly? (Review section 5.)
7. Does each sentence begin with a capital letter?
8. Does each name begin with a capital letter?
9. Are commas used where they are needed?
10. Is each paragraph indented? Is the form of the paragraphs correct?

Make corrections in your second draft. Then, write a final draft of your essay on a clean piece of paper. Give your final draft to your teacher.

10 MORE WRITING

Follow your teacher's instructions, or work on this section on your own if you have time.

1. Bring a photograph, magazine picture, or sketch of people to class. Discuss it with your partner. Write an essay about the people in it. Then, work with your classmates. Put your photographs or pictures on the wall of your classroom. Read each other's essays. Can you guess which essay is about which photograph or picture? If you can't, try to help each other to rewrite your essays.
2. Look out your classroom window, or go outside with your teacher. What are the people doing? Write a short essay about them.
3. Choose a character in a book or a movie. Write a short essay that describes this person. Write about the character's physical characteristics *and* what kind of person he or she is.

CHAPTER 5

Writing About the Future

Topic: Trips and plans

Rhetorical Focus: Chronological organization

Mechanical Focus: Sentence word order

Grammatical Focus: *going to* future tense; *be supposed to*; direct and indirect objects; *here/there* for places; *by* plus the method of transportation; *can*

Connectors and Transitions: Using pronouns for direct and indirect objects

---

1 PRE-WRITING: PUTTING EVENTS IN THE CORRECT SEQUENCE

Look at the pictures on the next page. They show what Fred is going to do next Tuesday.

Discuss the pictures with your partner. Then, decide with your partner the sequence in which the events are going to take place. Number the pictures according to this sequence. Use (1) for the first event, use (2) for the second event, and so on. Be prepared to explain the reasons for your choices to your classmates.

Is it possible to put the events in different sequences?

2 WRITING SENTENCES

**Look at this picture of Fred. Then, write
answers to the following questions.
Write complete sentences.**

1. Can you see Fred? Where is he?

   _____

   _____

2. What is he doing?

   _____

   _____

3. What is he going to do?

   _____

   _____

4. Is he going to travel? How?

   _____

   _____

5. Where is he going to go?

   _____

   _____

6. What is he going to do there?

   _____

   _____

3 GRAMMAR

A THE *GOING TO* FUTURE TENSE

> When you want to talk or write about the future, you can often use the *going to* future.

Subject	*to be*	*going to*	Simple Form of Verb
I	am	going to	cat.
You	are	going to	drive.
He	is	going to	fly.
She	is	going to	cook.
It	is	going to	rain.
We	are	going to	run.
You	are	going to	walk.
They	are	going to	sleep.

Fill in the blanks.

1. The *going to* future tense consists of the correct present form of the verb

   _____ plus _____ plus the simple form of the

   _____ .

EXERCISE 1

Here are some sentences about the present. Change them to sentences about the future. The first two are done for you.

1. I am writing in my book.

   I am going to write in my book.

2. You are reading your book.

   You are going to read your book.

3. They are studying English.

_____

4. I am looking at Fred.

_____

5. Fred is taking a taxi.

_____

6. Our mother is baking a birthday cake.

_____

7. We are talking about the lesson.

_____

EXERCISE 2

Fred likes to work in his garden on weekends. The following paragraph is about what he is going to do next Saturday. It contains blank spaces and the simple forms of verbs. Fill in each blank with the correct _going to_ form of the verb in parentheses. The first one is done for you.

Fred _is going to open_ (open) the left front door of his car.

He _____ (drive) to the store. At the

store, he _____ (buy) some vegetable

seeds. He _____ (come) back home. He

_____ (plant) the vegetable seeds in his

back yard. In a few months, he _____ (have) a

lot of fresh vegetables.

B   USING *HERE* AND *THERE* AS SUBSTITUTES FOR LOCATIONS

> When we use two sentences that talk about *the same location*, we can substitute *here* or *there* for the location in the second sentence.
>
> 1. My classmate is going to visit me *at my apartment*. He is going to come **here** at six o'clock.
> 2. Linda and her husband are going to take a trip *to Europe*. They are going to go **there** next summer.

Answer these questions.

1. Which word is used for the place where the speaker or writer is?

   here _____   *there* _____

2. Which word is used for a different place?

   here _____   *there* _____

EXERCISE 3

Fill in each blank with *here* or *there*.

1. This is a good university. I am going to study _____ for a year.

2. I am going to go home next summer. I am going to travel _____ by plane.

3. I am studying in Boston. My cousin is going to come _____ next month.

4. Our friends are going to go to Connecticut this weekend. They are going to travel _____ by car.

C USING *BY* PLUS THE METHOD OF TRANSPORTATION

We use *by* plus the method of transportation to tell *how* someone is going to travel somewhere.

1. How are you going to go back home today?
   I'm going to go there *by bus*.
2. How is your friend going to travel here?
   She's going to travel here *by train*.

EXERCISE 4

Ask your partner the following questions. Write your partner's answers. Write complete sentences.

1. How are you going to get home today?

   _____

   _____

2. How are you going to return to your country?

   _____

   _____

3. How are you going to travel to _____ next weekend?

   _____

   _____

D *BE SUPPOSED TO*

We use *be supposed to* plus the simple form of the verb to talk or write about events that are *scheduled* or *expected*. *Be supposed to* is less definite than *be going to*. Events that are supposed to happen may not occur.

1. The weather report says that it *is supposed to rain*, but I think it is going to be sunny.
2. It *is supposed to be* cold today. Are you going to wear your coat?
3. Linda and Fred *are supposed to meet* me at seven o'clock. I hope they are not going to be late.

EXERCISE 5

Fill in each blank with the correct form of *be supposed to* plus the simple form of the verb in parentheses.

1. I _____ (be) at school at

   nine o'clock, but I'm going to be late.

2. I am going to go home now because my classmate _____

   _____ (come) to my apartment in an hour.

3. We are studying now because we _____

   _____ (have) a test tomorrow.

E DIRECT AND INDIRECT OBJECTS

In English, *transitive verbs* are verbs that take *direct objects*. Here are some examples of transitive verbs plus direct objects.

1. I'm going to *do my homework.*
2. We're going to *bake a cake.*
3. Linda is going to *mail a letter.*

> **Some transitive verbs take *two objects*. The *direct object* shows the thing (or person) that directly receives the action of the verb. The *indirect object* shows the person (or thing) that in some way receives the direct object.**

Subject	Verb	Indirect Object	Direct Object
I	am going to give	**my teacher**	*a present.*
We	are supposed to bake	**Fred**	*a cake.*
We	are going to show	**you**	*the pictures.*

EXERCISE 6

**In the following sentences, draw a box around the indirect object.
Draw a line under the direct object. The first one is done for you.**

1. When are you going to show the teacher your paragraph?

2. Are you going to give your sister a present?

3. We are supposed to make Fred dinner.

4. Are you ready? I am going to throw you the ball.

5. I'm going to give you the keys because I'm going to get home very late.

EXERCISE 7

**Unscramble the following sentences, which contain direct and indirect
objects. The first one is done for you.**

1. mother, is, baking, her, cake, Mary's, a

    Mary's mother is baking her a cake.

2. I, buy, going, am, a, them, to, present

    _____

    _____

3. Fred, pictures, showing, us, his, is

    _____

    _____

4. are, give, they, Fred, book, going, a, to

    _____

    _____

5. is, the, asking, a, teacher, students, question, the

_____

_____

6. reading, her, Linda, a, is, daughter, story

_____

_____

F THE MODAL *CAN*

Can followed by the simple form of the verb is used to express possibility or ability.		
Subject	***Can* + Verb**	**Rest of the Sentence**
I	**can see**	Fred in the picture.
You	**can take**	a taxi to the airport.
He	**cannot come**	to Connecticut early.
She	**can meet**	Fred after the meeting.
It	**can't snow**	in London in August.
We	**can drive**	to Connecticut with you.
You	**can get**	home in a few hours.
They	**can walk**	to school.

Answer the following questions.

1. What are the two negative forms of *can*?

_____ and _____

Which one is the contraction? _____

2. Does *can* change its form according to the subject?   yes _____ no _____

3. What form of the verb comes after *can*?   _____

EXERCISE 8

Look at the pictures in section 1. Then, work with your partner to write and answer questions about Fred with *can* and the verb in parentheses. Use your imagination. The first two are done for you.

1. (drive) _Can Fred drive a car?_

   Yes, he can.

2. (pilot an airplane) _Can Fred pilot an airplane?_

   No, he cannot.

3. (speak Portuguese) _____

   _____

   _____

4. (cook) _____

   _____

   _____

5. (take a plane to his meeting) _____

   _____

   _____

EXERCISE 9

Now, ask your teacher, partner, or other classmates five questions with *can*. Then, write sentences based on their answers.

1. _____

   _____

2. _____

   _____

3. _____

_____

_____

4. _____

_____

_____

5. _____

_____

_____

4 EDITING

Proofread the sentences that your partner wrote in section 2 of this lesson. Ask your partner to proofread your sentences.

1. Does each sentence begin with a capital letter and end with a period?
2. Are commas used correctly?
3. Does each part of a name begin with a capital letter?
4. Are the forms of the *going to* future correct? (Review section 3A.)
5. Are other verb forms correct?
6. Are *here* and *there* used correctly? (Review section 3B.)
7. Is *by* used correctly? (Review section 3C.)
8. Is *be supposed to* used correctly? (Review section 3D.)
9. Are objects in the correct position in the sentences? (Review section 3E.)
10. Is *can* used correctly? (Review section 3F.)

Return your partner's sentences. Look at your partner's corrections of your sentences. Copy your corrected sentences onto a clean piece of paper, and give them to your teacher.

5 CONNECTORS AND TRANSITIONS

USING PRONOUNS AS DIRECT OBJECTS

Compare the following sentences.

Subject	Verb	Indirect Object	Direct Object (Noun)
Fred	is baking	**Linda**	*a pie.*
They	are going to tell	**the child**	*the story.*

Subject	Verb	Direct Object (Pronoun)	Indirect Object
Fred	is baking	*it*	**for Linda.**
They	are going to tell	*it*	**to the child.**

Answer these questions.

1. What kinds of direct objects occur after the indirect object?

   nouns _____ pronouns _____

2. What kinds of direct objects *must* occur before the indirect object?

   nouns _____ pronouns _____

3. When a direct object comes before the indirect object, what words occur

   before the indirect object? _____ and _____

EXERCISE 1

Read the sentences on the next page. Underline the direct objects.
Then, rewrite each sentence using a pronoun as the direct object.

Don't forget to change the word order and put a preposition before the indirect object. The first one is done for you.

1. Linda is going to give her father a <u>birthday card.</u>

   Linda is going to give it to her father.

2. We are going to show our teacher our paragraphs.

   _____

   _____

3. I am going to make my friend a sandwich.

   _____

   _____

4. Fred is buying his wife a present.

   _____

   _____

5. When are you going to give him the books?

   _____

   _____

6. Please tell us the story.

   _____

   _____

EXERCISE 2

The words in parentheses in the paragraph are indirect objects followed by direct objects. Fill in each blank with the indirect and direct objects in the correct order. Use a preposition if one is necessary. Then, copy the paragraph neatly onto a piece of lined paper.

Fred's birthday is next month. His children are going to

give _____

(him/some photographs). Right now, they are taking pictures.

When the pictures are developed, they are going to show

_____ (their

mother/them). She is going to give _____

_____ (them/advice). She is going to tell

them which pictures are the best. Then, they are to buy a

frame for the pictures. They are going to put the pictures in

the frame. They are going to give _____

_____ (their father/them).

6 GETTING READY TO WRITE A PARAGRAPH

A CHRONOLOGICAL ORGANIZATION

Chronological organization means putting events in the order in which they happened or are going to happen. In the paragraph about Fred, chronological organization is used. It starts in the present and tells what Fred is doing. Then, it tells about what Fred is going to do afterward, in the future. The future events are also in chronological order.

> Fred is going to take a plane. Then, he's going to go to a meeting. He's going to give a presentation there. After that, people are going to ask him questions, and he's going to answer them. Finally, he's going to return by plane and get home in time for dinner.

EXERCISE

On the next page there are some sentences about the future. Work with your partner to put them in correct *chronological order*. Then, copy the sentences in the space provided.

1. First, I'm going to go to France, and then I'm going to visit Italy.
2. I'm going to spend one month in Paris and another month in southern France.
3. After my vacation, I'm going to return to the United States.
4. I'm going to take a long vacation next summer.
5. I'm going to visit several Italian cities.
6. I'm going to spend two months in France.
7. Then, I'm going to spend one month in Italy.

Next Summer

_____

_____

_____

_____

_____

_____

_____

_____

_____

B ASKING AND ANSWERING QUESTIONS ABOUT NEXT WEEKEND

Here are some examples of questions and answers about next weekend.

Questions About Next Weekend

1. What's the weather going to be like next weekend?
2. Are you going to go anywhere? Where are you going to go? How are you going to go there?
3. What are you going to do? Why?
4. What are you going to do after that?

Answers to the Questions About Next Weekend

1. It's supposed to rain next weekend.
2. Yes, I am. I'm going to go to Connecticut. I'm going to drive.
3. I'm going to visit my parents and help them cook and clean because Sunday is my brother's birthday.
4. After that, I'm going to return to Boston.

Have a discussion with your partner about your plans for next weekend. Ask and answer questions. Write your questions for your partner. Write down your answers to your partner's questions.

Questions for My Partner About Next Weekend

_____

_____

_____

_____

Answers to My Partner's Questions About Next Weekend

_____

_____

_____

_____

7 WRITING A PARAGRAPH

Use the answers that you wrote in section 6 to write a paragraph about next weekend. Remember to put your sentences in chronological order.

Here is how the examples in section 6 can be used to write a paragraph.

Next Weekend

It's supposed to rain in Boston next weekend. I'm going to go to Connecticut. I'm going to drive there. I'm going to visit my parents and help them cook and clean because Sunday is my brother's birthday. On Monday, I'm going to return to Boston.

Next Weekend

_____

_____

_____

_____

_____

_____

_____

_____

8 EXPANDING YOUR PARAGRAPH

A ANSWERING MORE QUESTIONS ABOUT YOUR PLANS FOR NEXT WEEKEND

Here is an example of more questions and answers based on the sample paragraph in section 7.

Questions About Plans for Next Weekend

1. Is it supposed to rain in Connecticut?
2. Are you going to drive your own car?
3. When are you going to leave Boston?

4. When are you going to get to Connecticut?
5. Is your brother going to be there?
6. What are you going to cook?

Answers to Questions About Plans for Next Weekend

1. No, it isn't supposed to rain there. It's supposed to be sunny.
2. No, I'm not going to drive my own car. I'm going to rent a car at the car rental agency near my school.
3. I'm going to leave here at around two o'clock on Friday.
4. I'm going to get there at around five.
5. No, my brother isn't going to be there then. He's going to get there late Saturday.
6. We're going to cook some of my brother's favorite food. My mother is going to bake a cake for him.

Ask more questions about your partner's plans for next weekend. Write your questions and give them to your partner. Then, write answers to each other's questions.

Questions for My Partner

_____

_____

_____

_____

_____

Answers to My Partner's Questions

_____

_____

_____

_____

_____

_____

_____

_____

_____

B   ADDING MORE INFORMATION ABOUT YOUR PLANS FOR NEXT WEEKEND

Now, read your original paragraph and the answers that you wrote to your partner's questions. On a clean piece of paper, write a short essay (at least three paragraphs) about your plans for next weekend.

Here is an example based on the sample paragraph in section 7. The new information is underlined.

It's supposed to rain in Boston next weekend. I'm going to drive to Connecticut and visit my parents. It's supposed to be sunny there.

I'm going to rent a car at the car rental agency near my school. I'm going to leave Boston at around two, and I'm going to get to Connecticut at around five.

I'm going to visit my family because Sunday is my brother's birthday. I'm going to help my parents cook and clean. We're going to cook some of my brother's favorite food. My mother is going to bake a cake for him.

My brother isn't going to be in Connecticut on Friday. He's going to get there late Saturday. We're going to

<u>celebrate his birthday on Sunday</u>. Then, I'm going to return

to Boston on Monday.

9 REVISING AND EDITING

A REVISING

Here is an example of how section 8B's short sample essay about next weekend can be expanded.

Read the longer essay. Compare it with the short essay. Discuss the two essays with your partner. Make a list of the extra information that is in the longer essay.

Next Weekend

It's supposed to rain in Boston next weekend, but I'm not upset because I'm not going to be here. I'm going to drive down to Connecticut and visit my family. It's supposed to be sunny there.

I'm going to visit my family because Sunday is my brother's birthday. He's going to be twenty-eight. I'm going to buy him a present after school on Friday. Then, I'm going to rent a car at the car rental agency near my school. I'm going to bring my suitcase with me, and I'm going to leave for Connecticut from the car rental agency. I'm going to leave Boston at around two, and I'm going to get to my parents' house at around five.

I'm going to relax and talk with my parents Friday night. Then, on Saturday morning, I'm going to help them get everything ready. We're going to clean the house and buy some of my brother's favorite food. We're going to cook the food, and my mother is going to bake him a birthday cake. We're going to hide it in the refrigerator.

My brother can't come to Connecticut on Friday. He's going to get there late Saturday. He's going to come by plane from California. On Saturday night, we're going to relax and talk with my brother. We're not going to tell him about our plans for his birthday. We're going to surprise him on Sunday. On Monday, I'm going to return to Boston.

Extra Information in the Longer Essay

_____

_____

_____

_____

_____

_____

You have written a short essay about your plans for next weekend in section 8. You can still continue to expand your essay. Read it again, and see what interesting information you can add. Let your partner read it again and ask you more questions. Then, rewrite your essay with the added information.

B   EDITING

Ask your partner to proofread your essay, and proofread your partner's essay.

1. Does each sentence begin with a capital letter and end with a period?
2. Are commas used correctly?
3. Does each part of a name begin with a capital letter?
4. Are the forms of the *going to* future correct? (Review section 3A.)
5. Are other verb forms correct?
6. Are *here* and *there* used correctly? (Review section 3B.)
7. Is *by* used correctly? (Review section 3C.)
8. Is *be supposed to* used correctly? (Review section 3D.)
9. Are objects in the correct position in the sentences? (Review section 3E.)
10. Is *can* used correctly? (Review section 3F.)
11. Is the form of the paragraphs correct?

Return your partner's essay. Look at your partner's corrections of your essay. Copy your corrected essay onto a clean piece of paper, and give it to your teacher.

10 MORE WRITING

Follow your teacher's instructions, or work on this section on your own if you have time.

1. What is your partner going to do next summer? Discuss your partner's plans, and write a short essay about them. Let your partner read the essay and add information. Then, write a second draft of the essay, and ask your partner to proofread it.
2. What are you going to do after your English course? Write a short essay about your plans.
3. What is the world going to be like in ten years? in fifty years? Use your imagination and write a short essay about the future.

CHAPTER 6

Describing Views

Topic: Surroundings and seasons

Rhetorical Focus: Spatial organization

Mechanical Focus: Using commas after initial prepositional phrases

Grammatical Focus: The simple present tense; coordinated predicates

Connectors and Transitions: Initial prepositional phrases; *a*, *an*, *some*, and *the*

1 PRE-WRITING: TAKING NOTES ABOUT A PICTURE OR A VIEW

You can take notes about a picture or a view. You can write down the different things that you see. When you take notes, you do not have to write complete sentences. Here are some notes about the picture on the next page.

in my bedroom	red brick building
sitting	four stories
looking out my window	church
fourth floor	the sky—light grayish blue
two trees	no clouds
	don't see the sun

Now, look out your classroom window. Take notes about what you see. Then, try to draw a simple picture of the view.

Notes About the View from My
Classroom Window

My Drawing of the View from My Classroom Window

2 WRITING SENTENCES

A USING NOTES TO WRITE SENTENCES

EXERCISE 1

You can use notes to help you to write sentences. In the following example, the words and phrases from the notes on the picture in section 1 have been put into groups. Study the three examples. Then, work with your partner. Rewrite each group as a sentence.

1. in my bedroom   sitting   looking out my window   fourth floor

   I am sitting in my bedroom and looking out my fourth-floor window.

2. two trees

3. red brick building   four stories

There is a four-story red brick building.
_____

4. church

_____

5. the sky   light grayish blue

_____

6. no clouds

There aren't any clouds.

7. don't see the sun

_____

Now, look at your notes on page 121. Put related words and phrases into groups. Then use your groups to write sentences.

My Sentences About the View from
My Classroom Window

_____
_____
_____
_____
_____
_____
_____
_____

B ADDING INFORMATION ABOUT LOCATION

EXERCISE 2

Most of the sentences in exercise 1 can be expanded by adding information about location. Add the information about location that is in parentheses to make a longer sentence. (The sentences are numbered as they were in exercise 1.) The first one is done for you.

2. There are two trees. (close to my fourth-floor window)

    There are two trees close to my fourth-floor window.

3. There is a four-story red brick building. (in back of the trees)

4. There is a church. (behind this building)

6. There aren't any clouds. (in the sky)

7. I don't see the sun. (from my window)

EXERCISE 3

In Chapter 4, you learned that the prepositional phrase can begin a sentence.

Rewrite each of the expanded sentences *beginning* with the location. Be sure to use a *comma* after the location. The first one is done for you.

2. *Close to my fourth-floor window, there are two trees.*

3. _____

4. _____

6. _____

7. _____

3 GRAMMAR

A THE SIMPLE PRESENT TENSE

In English, there are *two present tenses.* One of them is the *present continuous tense,* which you practiced in Chapter 4. The other present tense is the *simple present tense.* It has two important uses in English.

1. It is used to show the present state of things using verbs that do not normally occur in the continuous.
2. It is used to show an action or state that is general or occurs regularly.

The simple present tense has the following forms.		
Subject	**Verb**	**Rest of the Sentence**
I	believe	you.
I	have	a cold.
You	look	tired.
You	have	a headache.
He	know**s**	that.
He	**has**	two brothers.
She	look**s**	good.
She	**has**	two brothers.
It	feel**s**	cold.
We	like	the book.
We	have	a car.

Check the correct answers.

1. How many parts does a simple present verb have?

   one _____ two _____

2. When the subject is *he, she,* or *it,* what is the last letter of the simple present verb?

   e _____ s _____

B THE SIMPLE PRESENT TENSE WITH VERBS THAT DO NOT NORMALLY OCCUR IN THE CONTINUOUS

Verbs that do not normally occur in the continuous usually fall into one of three categories.	
Category	**Examples of Verbs**
Verbs that indicate **possession** or **state** The church *has* a slanted roof.	*have, own*
Verbs that indicate **appearance** From here, the two trees *look* like one tree.	*appear, look, seem*
Verbs that indicate **perception, thought, knowledge,** or **feeling** I *don't see* the sun from my window, but I *know* it is there because of the yellow light that is bathing everything that I *see*.	*believe, hear, know, like, see, think*

EXERCISE 1

The following paragraphs are about things that are happening now. Fill in each blank with either the simple present or the present continuous form of the verb in parentheses.

It is autumn in Boston. The leaves on the trees _____

_____ (begin) to turn orange, red, and yellow. The

trees _____ (look) very different from

before. In fact, many things _____ (seem)

different from in the summer.

The air _____ (feel) a little cold.

People _____ (not, wear) summer clothes

now. They _____ (wear) brightly colored

autumn clothes. I really _____ (like) the

bright colors of the leaves and the clothes. I _____

_____ (have) a slight cold, but I am happy because it is

autumn.

C NEGATIVE FORMS OF THE SIMPLE PRESENT TENSE

Here are examples of negative forms of the simple present tense.

Subject	Verb	Rest of the Sentence
I	**do not like**	winter.
You	**don't own**	that car.
He	**does not have**	the book.
She	**doesn't look**	sick.
It	**doesn't seem**	like morning.
We	**do not hear**	any music.
You	**don't have**	a bicycle.
They	**don't see**	us.

Answer the following questions.

1. What two words occur before the simple form of the verb when the subject is *I, you, we,* or *they*? _____

2. What two words occur before the simple form of the verb when the subject is *he, she,* or *it*? _____

3. What is the contraction of *do not*? _____

4. What is the contraction of *does not*? _____

EXERCISE 2

The first sentence in each pair contains a present continuous or simple present verb. Fill in the blank in the second sentence in each pair with the correct negative form of the verb. The first two are done for you.

1. They are wearing autumn clothes. They _____*aren't wearing*_____ summer clothes.

2. She has three brothers. She _____*doesn't have*_____ any sisters.

3. I like autumn. I _____ winter.

4. We are studying English. We _____ Italian.

5. He looks tired. He _____ sick.

6. You see a bird. You _____ an airplane.

7. It feels sunny. It _____ warm.

8. She is baking a cake. She _____ a pie.

9. I hear Fred. I _____ Linda.

10. We know Karen. We _____ her parents.

D USING THE SIMPLE PRESENT TENSE TO SHOW AN ACTION OR STATE THAT IS GENERAL, OR AN ACTION THAT OCCURS REGULARLY

The simple present tense is also used to show an action or state that is general or occurs regularly. Here are some examples.

> The tops of the trees *come* up to the middle of my window. (This is a general state. It is not something that is true only now.)
>
> The people are inside now because it is winter. In the warm weather, they often *sit* outside and *talk* and *eat*. (These are actions that occur regularly in the warm weather.)

EXERCISE 3

Fill in each blank in the following short essay with the correct simple present form of the verb in parentheses. Look up any words that you do not know in your dictionary, or ask your teacher to explain them to you.

Spring is the season between winter and summer. In

Boston, it is supposed to start in late March or early April,

but it sometimes _____ (not, start) until

May. It is supposed to finish at the end of June, but it

sometimes _____ (finish) in early June. It

is my favorite season. Perhaps I _____

(like) it so much because it is often a very short season.

When spring _____ (begin), the

weather _____ (get) warm. If there is any

snow on the ground, it _____ (melt).

The sky _____ (become) sunny, and

the days _____ (become) longer. Green

leaves _____ (appear) on trees, and

flowers _____ (start) to blossom.

People _____ (take) off their winter coats

and _____ (put) on their spring clothes.

Bright and colorful scenery _____

(replace) the monotonous views of winter.

During spring, there are sometimes some cold days.

Sometimes, nature _____ (fool) us and

there is even some snow. However, these tricks _____

_____ (not, spoil) spring for me. I _____

(know) that the snow is going to melt, and new flowers are

going to appear. Even if a particular spring is short and cold,

summer _____ (start) quickly in Boston.

The limited days of spring are very precious to me.

I _____ (know) that once the hot weather

_____ (begin) I am going to miss spring.

E COORDINATED PREDICATES

Study the following groups of sentences with your partner. For each group, discuss how the two sentences on the left are combined to make the sentence on the right. Then answer the questions that come after the sentences.

1. I am sitting in my bedroom.

   I am looking out my fourth-floor window.

   I am sitting in my bedroom and looking out my fourth-floor window.

2. People take off their winter coats.

   People put on their spring clothes.

   People take off their winter coats and put on their spring clothes.

3. Karen is standing on a hill.

   Karen is looking at everything she can see.

   Karen is standing on a hill and looking at everything she can see.

4. This summer, we are going to drive home.

   This summer, we are going to visit our families.

   This summer, we are going to drive home and visit our families.

1. Underline the words that each pair of sentences on the left has in common.
2. How many times do these words occur in the sentence on the right?
3. Is there a comma before *and* in the sentence on the right?
4. Write a rule for combining sentences like those on the left to make sentences like those on the right.

_____

_____

_____

_____

EXERCISE 4

Combine each pair of sentences to make a new sentence with a coordinated predicate.

1. We are sitting in our classroom.

   _____

   _____

   _____

   _____

   We are listening to our teacher.

2. The snow looks clean.

   _____

   _____

   _____

   _____

   The snow feels cold.

3. I see the people on the street.

   _____

   _____

   _____

   _____

   I hear the birds in the trees.

4. It's going to rain tomorrow.

_____

_____

_____

_____

It's going to be cold
tomorrow.

_____

4 EDITING

A EXPANDING SENTENCES

Now, look at the sentences you wrote in section 2 about the view
from your classroom window. Show them to your partner. Let your
partner ask you questions. Decide how to expand the sentences. For
example, you can add information about location. On a clean piece of
paper, rewrite your sentences with the expansions.

B PROOFREADING

Proofread your partner's sentences, and ask your partner to
proofread your sentences.

1. Are the simple present and present continuous tenses used correctly?
   (Review sections 3A, B, C, and D.)
2. Are the forms of each verb correct? Are there *-s* endings on simple
   present verbs that go with *he*, *she*, and *it*? (Review section 3A.)
3. Are the sentences that contain coordinated predicates correct? (Review
   section 3E.)

Copy your corrected sentences onto a clean piece of paper, and give
them to your teacher.

5 CONNECTORS AND TRANSITIONS

A USING *A*, *AN*, *THE*, AND *SOME* TO CONNECT SENTENCES

Read the following paragraph. Underline the words *a*, *an*, *the*, and *some*.

     Karen is standing on a hill and looking at everything that she can see. Right below the hill, there is a narrow road. The road leads to a small farm. Around the farm, there is an old fence. There are some chickens inside the fence. The chickens are very small, but Karen still sees them.

Work with your partner. Discuss the following questions:

1. What is the difference between *a* and *an*?
2. What is the difference between *a* and *some*?
3. What word comes before a noun that has been mentioned before?

EXERCISE 1

Fill in each blank in the following paragraph with *a*, *an*, *some*, or *the*.
Be prepared to explain the reasons for your choice.

Carl is sitting at _____ table in his school cafeteria. He is

reading _____ book for his next class. He is also drinking

_____ cup of coffee. There are _____ other students at

_____ table. One of them is eating _____ hamburger.

_____ hamburger really smells good. In fact, all of _____

other students are eating. Carl is getting very hungry. He's

probably going to get lunch soon.

B ANOTHER USE OF THE DEFINITE ARTICLE

> **The definite article *the* is also used before nouns that refer to objects that are unique (there is only one of them) or to objects that are unique in a particular place.**
>
> 1. I am looking out **the** window. (*There may be only one window in the bedroom.*)
> 2. **The** sky is light grayish blue. (*There is only one sky.*)
> 3. I don't see **the** sun from my window. (*There is only one sun.*)

EXERCISE 2

Fill in each blank in the following paragraph with *a*, *an*, *some*, or *the*.

_____ ceiling in my bedroom is cracked. Whenever I lie

in bed and look at it, I imagine that I see different things.

Right now, I think that I see _____ mountains. It is winter, and there are _____ people skiing on them. _____ sky is

clear, and _____ sun is shining, but it is very cold. _____

people are wearing warm clothes. I think they are going to sit

around _____ orange fire when they finish skiing.

6 GETTING READY TO WRITE A PARAGRAPH

    (1) I am sitting in my bedroom and looking out the
window. (2) Close to my fourth-floor window, there are two
trees. (3) In back of the trees, there is a four-story red brick
building. (4) Behind this building, there is a church. (5) The
sky is light grayish blue, and there are not any clouds. (6) I
don't see the sun from my window.

**Discuss the paragraph with your partner. Talk about the order in
which the things that the writer sees are described. In each of the
circles on the picture, put in the number of the sentence that tells
about the object or what is happening. Then, draw a line connecting**

the circles. Start with (1) and finish with (5). You can't label anything (6), because the sun isn't in the picture. Is the line relatively straight?

This paragraph is an example of the use of spatial organization. The sentences in the paragraph are organized according to the position of things in *space*.

EXERCISE

Here are some sentences that can be made into a paragraph. Work with your partner. Put the sentences in *spatial order* to make a well-organized paragraph. Then, make a simple drawing of the scene that is described. Number each part of the drawing according to the order of your sentences. Is your spatial organization good?

1. Past the tall buildings, I see the highway that surrounds the city.
2. Across the river, there is another city.
3. I am standing at the top of a tall building and looking at the view.
4. There is a wide river next to the highway.
5. Around the building, there are other tall buildings.

7 WRITING A PARAGRAPH

On a clean piece of paper, write a short paragraph about the view from your classroom window, the view from your window at home, or a street scene near your home. Use spatial organization.

8 EXPANDING YOUR PARAGRAPH

Work with your partner to expand your paragraph. Begin by writing each sentence from your paragraph on a separate card or piece of paper. Give your cards to your partner. Let your partner write questions that ask for more information. Then, write answers to your partner's questions.

On the next page there is an example of how some of the cards might look for the paragraph in section 6.

Close to my fourth-floor window, there are two trees.

Are the trees close to each other?

Yes, they are.

How tall are they?

They are fairly tall. Their tops come up to the middle of my window.

What do they look like?

Their trunks are not very wide, and they are gray and dusty.

What do their leaves look like?

They are small, dry, and yellowish.

After you answer your partner's questions, use the extra information on each of your cards to write a paragraph. Then, combine the paragraphs to make an essay. (You may want to keep your first and second sentences in the same paragraph.)

Here is an example of how the paragraph in section 6 could be expanded. (The sentences from the original paragraph are highlighted.)

It is winter in Boston. **I am sitting in my bedroom and looking out the window.** The most striking thing is that nothing is green. **Close to my fourth-floor window, there are two trees.** They are very close to each other, so from here they look like one tree. They are fairly tall. Their tops come up to the middle of my window. However, their trunks are not very wide, so they are probably about thirty years old. Their trunks are gray and dusty, but the February sun is giving them a yellowish appearance. They have small, dry leaves at the tips of their branches. These also look yellowish because of the sun.

In back of the trees, there is a four-story red brick building. There is a wooden balcony attached to the building. The wood is old and light brown, and it also has a yellowish cast because of the sun. I see just one corner of the balcony. On it, there is a small wooden table. There aren't any people at it, but in the warm weather people often sit there and talk and eat. Right now, there is still snow from the last storm on the balcony. There is also snow on the flat roof of the building.

Behind this building, there is a church. It is also a brick building, but the color of the bricks is different. They are light orange. The church has a slanted roof, and there is not any snow on it.

The sky is light grayish blue, and there are not any clouds. I don't see the sun from my window, but I know it is there because of the yellow light that is bathing everything that I see.

9 REVISING AND EDITING

A REVISING

Read your partner's essay, and let your partner read your essay. Number the paragraphs in your partner's essay. Then, in the space provided, draw a simple sketch of the view that your partner writes about. Put the number of each paragraph near the part of the sketch that it describes. Then, connect the numbers with a line. Is the line relatively straight? Is the essay spatially well organized?

The View That My Partner Describes

You and your partner can discuss the spatial organization of your essays with each other. Make suggestions for changing the organization if this is necessary. You can also make suggestions about adding or leaving out information. Then, write a second draft of your essay according to the suggestions that you agree with.

B   EDITING

Proofread your partner's second draft, and ask your partner to proofread your second draft.

1. Are the simple present and present continuous tenses used correctly? (Review sections 3A, B, C, and D.)
2. Is the form of each verb correct? Are there -s endings on simple present verbs that go with *he, she,* and *it*? (Review section 3A.)
3. Are *a, an, some,* and *the* used correctly? (Review section 5.)

10   MORE WRITING

Follow your teacher's instructions, or work on this section on your own if you have time.

1. Choose a painting from a museum or a book. Write a short essay that describes the painting.
2. Choose a small section of the university you are attending or the town or city that you are living in now. Write a short essay to describe this section to a friend who has never been there.
3. Relax and close your eyes. Imagine that you are in a special place where you feel relaxed and happy. Imagine that you are walking in this place, moving from one place to another. Continue walking and observing the place for as long as you feel comfortable. Then, open your eyes. Write a short essay that describes your special place. Try to show why it is special to you. You may want to relax and "return" to the place to make more observations.

CHAPTER 7

Writing About a Past Experience

Topic: A dangerous or frightening experience

Rhetorical Focus: Chronological order

Mechanical Focus: Using commas after chronological connectors and adverbs of manner

Grammatical Focus: The simple past tense; adverbs of manner; verbs that are followed by infinitives

Connectors and Transitions: Chronological connectors; words that show cause and effect

1 PRE-WRITING: PUTTING SENTENCES IN CHRONOLOGICAL ORDER

Look at the sentences Linda wrote on the next page. They are about part of a trip that she and her family took to California. The events that the sentences describe took place after the family stopped to get some sleep in a Howard Johnson's parking lot in Kansas. They are *not* in chronological order.

Work with your partner to put them in chronological order. Put a (1) next to the first sentence, a (2) next to the second, and so on. Be prepared to explain your order to your classmates. Are different orders possible?

_____ I went back to the car.

_____ My husband and children went to sleep, but I couldn't sleep because there was sheet lightning.

_____ After a while, the storm stopped suddenly.

_____ In the Howard Johnson's, there was a young man.

_____ Therefore, I decided to go into the Howard Johnson's for a cup of coffee.

_____ We drove to a gas station to get gas for the car.

_____ I asked him about the sheet lightning, and he told me not to worry about it.

_____ We quickly woke up our children and began to carry and push them into the gas station.

_____ I woke up my husband, and he decided to continue driving.

_____ Suddenly, a terrible storm started.

_____ Then, things got even worse.

2 WRITING SENTENCES

Can you remember an exciting, dangerous, or frightening experience? Tell your partner about it. Then, write full-sentence answers to these questions.

Answers to Questions About My Dangerous or Frightening Experience

1. Where and when did the experience occur?

_____

_____

_____

2. What happened?

_____

_____

_____

_____

_____

3. What happened after that?

_____

_____

_____

Here are Linda's answers.

1. The incident happened in a Howard Johnson's parking lot in Kansas. It happened when my family and I were on our way from Boston to California.
2. I tried to sleep, but sheet lightning kept me awake. I went into the Howard Johnson's. Someone there told me not to worry. But after I got

back to the car, there was a terrible storm. We drove to a gas station and stayed inside it.

3. We left the gas station and had breakfast. Then, we continued on our way to California.

Read your partner's answers, and let your partner read your answers. Then, write more questions for each other. Write short answers to the questions.

Here are Linda's answers to some questions.

1. What time did the incident occur?
   at around three o'clock in the morning
2. Why did you stop?
   because my husband was tired
3. Why did you go into the Howard Johnson's?
   because I couldn't sleep
4. Who told you not to worry?
   a young man
5. Why did you go to the gas station?
   because my husband wanted to buy gas
6. What happened there?
   the storm got even worse
7. How did the storm stop?
   suddenly
8. Where did you go for breakfast?
   to the Howard Johnson's
9. How did you feel?
   relieved

My Partner's
Questions and My Answers

_____

_____

_____

_____

_____

_____

Now, use Linda's short answers to write complete sentences. The first one is done for you.

More Sentences
About Linda's Experience

1. *The incident occurred at around three o'clock in the morning.*

2.

3.

4.

5.

6.

7.

8.

9.

Now, use your short answers to write more sentences about your experience.

More Sentences
About My Experience

3 GRAMMAR

A THE SIMPLE PAST TENSE OF *TO BE*

When we want to talk or write about the past in English, the most common tense is the *simple past*.

The simple past of the verb *to be* is irregular.

Subject	Simple Past of *to be*	Rest of the Sentence
I	was	afraid of the lightning.
You	were	on your way to California.
He	was	very tired.
She	was	not in the car.
It	was	summer.
We	were	on our way.
You	were	not in the restaurant.
They	were	in the restaurant.

Answer these questions.

1. What simple past form of *to be* is used with *you*, *we*, and *they*?

   _____

2. What simple past form of *to be* is used with *I*, *he*, *she*, and *it*? _____

EXERCISE 1

Rewrite the following sentences to contain past forms of the verb *to be*. Add the word or words in parentheses. The first one is done for you.

1. It is hot. ___*It was hot yesterday.*_____(yesterday)

2. The family is not in California _____

   _____ (this morning)

3. They are not in Boston. _____

_____ (last week)

4. You are in the United States. _____

_____ (last month)

5. I am not very tired. _____

_____ (this morning)

6. Their mother is in the restaurant. _____

_____ (until eleven
o'clock last night)

7. We are in Boston. _____

_____ (last summer)

B COULD AS THE PAST OF CAN

> The simple past of the verb *can* is the same for all subjects:
> *could*.

EXERCISE 2

**Rewrite the sentences that contain *can* as past sentences with *could*.
Add the words in parentheses to your past sentences. The first one is
done for you.**

1. I can see the sun from my window. *I could see the sun from my window yesterday.*

_____ (yesterday)

2. Linda can speak a little Spanish. _____

_____ (last year)

3. Her husband can drive for a long time without stopping. _____

_____ (when they went to California)

4. I can see a man in front of the restaurant. _____

_____ (in my dream)

C THE SIMPLE PAST TENSE OF REGULAR VERBS

Here are examples of the simple past of regular verbs.		
Subject	**Verb**	**Rest of the Sentence**
I	ask**ed**	him a question.
You	stay**ed**	in the car.
He	start**ed**	to drive.
She	look**ed**	out the window.
It	happen**ed**	in Kansas.
We	talk**ed**	in the restaurant.
You	open**ed**	the car door.
They	yawn**ed**	because they were tired.

Answer these questions.

1. Is the simple past form the same for all subjects? yes _____   no _____

2. What two letters are added to the simple form of regular verbs to make

   the simple past? _____

Sometimes, the spelling of regular simple past verbs is slightly irregular. You can tell how to spell a simple past regular verb if you know how to spell the base, or simple form. You can find the simple form in your dictionary.

Spelling Rules for Regular Simple Past Verbs		
Category	**Rule**	**Examples**
Verbs that end in the letter **e**	Add **-d**	continue/**continued** decide/**decided**
Verbs that end in the letter **y** preceded by a consonant	Change the **y** to **i**. Add **-ed**.	try/**tried** study/**studied** carry/**carried**
Verbs that have one syllable and end in a single vowel followed by a single consonant	Double the consonant. Add **-ed.**	stop/**stopped** plan/**planned**
Verbs that have more than one syllable and end in a stressed syllable with a single vowel followed by a single consonant	Double the consonant. Add **-ed.**	occur/**occurred**

EXERCISE 3

The following paragraph is about the future. Change it into a paragraph about the past. Change the future verbs to simple past verbs. Write the paragraph on a clean piece of paper.

Linda is going to visit her parents next Friday. They are going to ask her about her trip to California. She is going to talk about her trip and show them some photographs. They are going to look at the photographs and ask her about them. When she talks about the tornado, she is going to start to get nervous. She is going to describe everything to them. After they talk, she is going to stay for dinner. After dinner, she is going to walk home.

Here is how to begin the paragraph in the past.

Linda visited her parents last Friday. They asked her about . . .

D IRREGULAR VERBS

Some of the most common verbs in English are irregular. They form the simple past in different ways. Like regular verbs, however, they are the same regardless of their subject.

Base Form	Sentence Containing an Irregular Simple Past
come	The children **came** home on time.
drink	They **drank** milk with their dinner.
drive	We **drove** to California with our children.
eat	The family **ate** in a restaurant last night.
get	They **got** up late yesterday.
go	We **went** to California several years ago.
have	We **had** breakfast early this morning.
sit	They **sat** near the window.
take	We **took** our children into the gas station.
tell	He **told** me not to worry.
wake	She **woke** up because of the lightning.

> **In this chapter and in later chapters, you will see other examples of irregular past verbs. Try to guess what the base form of the verb is. Then, check your guess by using a dictionary. If you are not sure, ask your partner or your teacher to help you.**

EXERCISE 4

Complete the following paragraphs by adding the correct simple past form of the verb in parentheses. Then, copy the paragraphs onto a clean piece of paper. The first two are done for you.

I _____*had*_____ (have) a bad dream last night. In the

dream, I _____*was*_____ (be) in a car. I _____ (be)

alone. I _____ (be) hungry, so I _____ (stop)

at a drive-in restaurant.

The restaurant _____ (be) dark and empty, but I

_____ (can, see) a waiter in front of it. He

_____ (tell) me that the restaurant _____

(be) closed. However, he _____ (take) my order. I

_____ (order) a hamburger and a glass of juice. He

_____ (go) into the restaurant and _____

(get) my order. Soon, he _____ (come) out and

_____ (knock) on the window of my car. He

_____ (give) me the hamburger and the juice. The

hamburger _____ (be) green, and the juice

_____ (be) blue. However, I _____ (be)

very hungry, so I _____ (sit) in the car and

_____ (eat) the hamburger and _____

(drink) the juice.

Suddenly, there _____ (be) a loud noise. The sky

_____ (turn) red, and the restaurant _____

(disappear). I _____ (drive) away quickly. Then my

car _____ (start) to shake. Then, I _____

(be) in a small boat on the ocean. At that point, I _____

(wake) up and _____ (realize) that it _____

(be) only a dream.

E NEGATIVE FORMS

Here are the negative simple past forms of the verb *to be*.

Subject	Negative Past of *to be*	Rest of the Sentence
I	was not	in the car.
You	weren't	in the restaurant.
He	wasn't	inside the restaurant.
She	wasn't	with me in the car.
It	wasn't	very cold in my dream.
We	were not	tired after the ride.
You	weren't	in California last year.
They	weren't	in my dream.

Answer these questions.

1. What word is added to make *was* and *were* negative? _____

2. Where is it added? before *was* and *were* _____ after *was* and *were* _____

3. What is the contraction of *was not?* _____

4. What is the contraction of *were not?* _____

> **The negative form of *could* is *could not*. The contraction is *couldn't*.**
>
> 1. Linda *could not* sleep because there was sheet lightning.
> 2. Her husband *couldn't* drive any more because he was tired.

> **All other simple past verbs form the negative by putting *did* plus *not* before the simple form of the verb.**
>
> | Subject | Negative Past | Rest of the Sentence |
> |---------|---------------|----------------------|
> | I | **did not get** | up early after my dream. |
> | You | **did not come** | to the restaurant. |
> | He | **didn't eat** | with us yesterday. |
> | She | **didn't drink** | all of the juice. |
> | It | **didn't rain** | in my dream. |
> | We | **didn't walk** | to the drive-in. |
> | You | **didn't try** | to talk to the waiter. |
> | They | **did not drive** | to the restaurant. |

Answer these questions.

1. What words are added to make all other verbs negative?_____

2. What is the form of the main verb in the negative simple past?

   past form _____   simple form _____

3. Where are *did* and *not* added?   before the simple form of the verb _____

   after the simple form of the verb _____

4. What is the contraction of *did not*? _____

EXERCISE 5

Change the affirmative verb in each sentence to a negative verb. Copy the sentences onto a clean piece of paper. The first two are done for you.

1. We were in Canada last year. We _____*weren't*_____ in the United States.

2. Mary drove to New York. She ___*didn't drive*___ to California.

3. I was on vacation last month. I _____ at school.

4. You came to the restaurant. You _____ to my house.

5. Linda could see the sheet lightning. Her children _____

it because they were asleep.

6. They took the bus to Washington. They _____ the

train.

7. Linda's husband went to Australia last year. Linda _____.

8. Linda could speak a little Spanish when she was a child. She

_____ any French.

9. It got cold yesterday afternoon. It _____ cloudy.

10. Linda ate a lot of toast at breakfast. She _____ any

eggs.

11. I had a headache before the storm. I _____ a fever.

12. They went to Niagara Falls, but they _____ to

Canada.

F   ADVERBS OF MANNER

Adverbs of manner modify a sentence or a verb (an action). They generally answer the question *how*.	
Sentence with an Adjective Describing a Noun	**Sentence with an Adverb Describing an Action**
Linda was *careful*.	Linda drove *carefully*. (How did she drive?)
My movements were *slow*.	I opened my eyes *slowly*. (How did I open my eyes?)
She is a *good* driver.	She drives *well*. (How does she drive?)

Answer these questions.

1. What two-letter suffix usually changes an adjective into an adverb of

   manner? _____

2. What is the irregular adverb of manner for the adjective *good?* _____

Adverbs of manner that end in *-ly* can generally occur in one of three positions in a sentence.

At the beginning of a sentence, followed by a comma:
1. **Suddenly**, a terrible storm started. (How did the terrible storm start?)

Between the subject and the verb:
2. We **quickly** woke up our children. (How did we wake up our children?)

At the end of a sentence:
3. After a while, the storm stopped **suddenly**. (How did the storm stop?)

EXERCISE 6

Work with your partner to fill in each blank with an appropriate *adverb of manner*. The first two are done for you.

I had a bad dream last night, so I didn't sleep ___*well*___.

It was hard for me to get up this morning. I opened my eyes

___*slowly*___ and rubbed them with my hands. Then, I got out

of bed _____ because I was a little dizzy.

I walked to the kitchen _____ and sat

down _____ at the table. I sat there for a

long time and didn't do anything. _____,

I looked at the clock. I had only fifteen minutes to get ready.

I jumped up _____, ran to the

bathroom, washed, and got dressed. _____,

I got my books and walked to the kitchen. I opened the

refrigerator _____ and poured myself a

glass of orange juice. Then, I _____

grabbed my keys and ran down the stairs to the bus stop.

When I got to school, I collapsed _____

in my seat and waited for the class to begin.

G   VERBS THAT ARE FOLLOWED BY INFINITIVES

Discuss these sentences with your partner.

1. I *decided to go* into the Howard Johnson's.
2. We *began to carry* our children into the gas station.

Fill in the blanks.

1. What form of the verb comes after *to*? _____

2. Which verb shows the past tense? the one before *to* ____ the one after

    to ____

3. What two words make up the infinitive? _____ and _____

Now, discuss these sentences.

1. I *am going to decide* **to go** into the Howard Johnson's.
   She *is going to decide* **to go** into the Howard Johnson's.
   They *are deciding* **to go** into the Howard Johnson's.
   He *decides* **to go** into the Howard Johnson's.
2. He *is beginning* **to carry** his children into the gas station.
   You *are going to begin* **to carry** your children into the gas station.
   They *begin* **to carry** their children into the gas station.
   She *begins* **to carry** her children into the gas station.

Fill in the blanks.

1. Does the infinitive form change according to the tense or subject?

    yes ____ no ____

2. Which verb changes to show tense and subject? _____

EXERCISE 7

The following paragraph is written in the present. Work with your partner to rewrite it in the simple past. Remember to change the form of the main verbs. Do not change the infinitives.

> Ping and his family plan to take a trip to Europe in July. They expect to leave on July first, and they want to return at the end of the month. They have to buy their airplane tickets in June. They also need to make sure that they have their passports on time. They don't want to take much cash with them, so they have to buy traveler's checks before they leave. They expect to have a good time in Europe because they are planning everything carefully.

Begin your paragraph as follows.

> Ping and his family planned to take a trip to Europe in July. They expected to . . .

4 EDITING

Proofread the sentences that your partner wrote in section 2. Ask your partner to proofread your sentences.

1. Are the past forms of the verb *to be* correct? (Review section 3A.)
2. Are the past forms of *can* correct? (Review section 3B.)
3. Are the past forms of regular verbs correct? (Review section 3C.)
4. Are the past forms of irregular verbs correct? (Review section 3D.)
5. Are the negative past forms correct? (Review section 3E.)
6. Are adverbs of manner used correctly? (Review section 3F.)
7. Are the infinitive forms used correctly? (Review section 3G.)

5 CONNECTORS AND TRANSITIONS

A WORDS AND PHRASES THAT EMPHASIZE CHRONOLOGICAL ORDER

Read the following paragraph based on Linda's answers in section 2.

> We stopped at about three o'clock in the morning for my husband to get some sleep in a Howard Johnson's parking lot

in Kansas. He and our children went to sleep, but I couldn't sleep because there was sheet lightning. Therefore, I decided to go into the Howard Johnson's for a cup of coffee. In the Howard Johnson's, there was a young man. I asked him about the sheet lightning, and he told me not to worry about it. I went back to the car. Suddenly, a terrible storm started. I woke up my husband, and he decided to continue driving. We drove to a gas station to get gas for the car. Then, things got even worse. We quickly woke up our children and began to carry and push them into the gas station. After a while, the storm stopped suddenly. Finally, we left the gas station and had breakfast at the Howard Johnson's.

Now, underline the sentences that begin with the words *then* and *finally* and the sentence that begins with the phrase *after a while*. These are used to emphasize that the events are written about in *chronological order*.

Answer these questions.

1. In this paragraph, what part of the sentence are the chronological

   connectors found in? The beginning _____ the middle _____ the end _____

2. What punctuation mark comes after each chronological connector?

   _____

Here are some other common chronological connectors.

after that	later
first	next

EXERCISE 1

Work with your partner. Read the sentences, and use your dictionary to look up any words you don't understand. Then, put the sentences in chronological order. Copy them onto a clean piece of paper in paragraph form. Use chronological connectors.

1. He went to the store and bought them.
2. He surprised her with the cake.
3. He looked in a cookbook for a good recipe.
4. He made a list of the ingredients.
5. Fred wanted to make a cake for Linda's birthday.

6. He needed flour, eggs, sugar, and vanilla.
7. He mixed the flour, eggs, sugar, and other ingredients in a large bowl to make a batter.
8. He checked in the kitchen to see what he already had.
9. He greased a pan.
10. He baked the cake for forty-five minutes.
11. He took it out and cooled it.
12. He poured the batter into the pan.

B WORDS THAT SHOW CAUSE AND EFFECT

Because

Generally, when we ask a question with *why* we expect an answer with *because*.

> **Why** couldn't you sleep?
> **Because** there was sheet lightning.

This is how *because* is often used in *speaking*. However, the group of words that begins with *because* is *not a complete sentence*.

In *writing*, we have to use complete sentences.

Result	**Cause**
I couldn't sleep	*because* there was sheet lightning.

This is *a complete sentence*. You can use sentences like this in *writing*.

Answer these questions.

1. Can the following group of words be used in writing? *Because I got up late.*

   yes _____ no _____

2. Can you and your partner write a complete sentence that contains this group of words?

   _____

3. In the sentence, *Fred baked a cake because it was Linda's birthday*, which group of words shows the cause?

   _____

Which group of words shows the result?

_____

EXERCISE 2

Combine the following questions and answers to make one complete sentence. The first two are done for you.

1. Why didn't you come on time?
   Because I got up late.

   I didn't come on time because I got up late.

2. Why is Linda happy?
   Because she visited her parents yesterday.

   Linda is happy because she visited her parents yesterday.

3. Why are you doing your homework?
   Because the teacher wants us to hand it in tomorrow.

   _____

   _____

4. Why are there clouds in the sky?
   Because it's going to rain soon.

   _____

   _____

5. Why didn't you bring an umbrella?
   Because I didn't know that it was going to rain.

   _____

   _____

6. Why did the people stop at a parking lot?
   Because the driver wanted to get some sleep.

   _____

   _____

7. Why did Linda wake up her husband?
Because a terrible storm started.

_____

_____

EXERCISE 3

Now, answer each of the following _why_ questions. Then, write a complete sentence that contains your answer. The first two are done for you.

1. Why did Linda and her husband wake up their children?

   Because the storm got even worse.

   Linda and her husband woke up their children because the storm got even worse.

2. Why did they leave the gas station?

   Because the storm stopped.

   They left the gas station because the storm stopped.

3. Why was our classmate absent last week?

   _____

   _____

   _____

4. Why are we going to have a test?

   _____

   _____

   _____

5. Why do you do some of your work with your partner?

   _____

   _____

   _____

6. Why is it hot in the summer?

_____

_____

_____

7. Why do people in most of the United States wear heavy clothes in the winter?

_____

_____

_____

8. Why did you decide to study English?

_____

_____

_____

Therefore

Another word that shows cause and result is *therefore*.
Cause   **Result**   I couldn't sleep.   *Therefore*, I decided to go into the   Howard Johnson's.

Answer these questions.

1. How many sentences does *therefore* connect? _____

2. What punctuation mark comes after *therefore*? _____

Both *because* and *therefore* can be used in sentences that are about cause and result. However, the order and punctuation are different.

Compare the following sentences.

I decided to go into the Howard Johnson's *because* I couldn't sleep.

    1. Which comes first?   the cause _____ the result _____

    2. How many sentences are there? _____

I couldn't sleep. *Therefore,* I decided to go into the Howard Johnson's.

    1. Which comes first?   the cause _____ the result _____

    2. How many sentences are there? _____

EXERCISE 4

Look at the sentences that you wrote with *because* in exercise 2. Now, change them into pairs of sentences that contain *therefore*. Write the new sentences. The first two are done for you.

    1. I didn't come on time because I got up late.

       I got up late. Therefore, I didn't come on time.

    2. Linda is happy because she visited her parents yesterday.

       Linda visited her parents yesterday. Therefore, she is happy.

    3. _____

       _____

    4. _____

       _____

    5. _____

       _____

    6. _____

       _____

    7. _____

       _____

6 GETTING READY TO WRITE A PARAGRAPH

Reread the sentences that you wrote in section 2. Discuss them with your partner, and put them in chronological order.

My Sentences About

in Chronological Order

_____

_____

_____

_____

_____

_____

_____

_____

_____

_____

_____

_____

7 WRITING A PARAGRAPH

Reread the paragraph about Linda's frightening experience in section 5A. Then use your chronological list of sentences from section 6 to write a paragraph about your experience. Write your paragraph on a clean piece of paper.

8 EXPANDING YOUR PARAGRAPH

THE THREE PARTS OF A NARRATIVE

Usually, when we tell or write a story, we spend most of our time talking about *the incident that we want to emphasize*. This is what Linda did in her paragraph about her frightening experience. However, the reader will also want to know about what happened before the incident and when and where it took place. This is called *background* information. This information can be given in a short paragraph that comes before the description of the incident.

The reader will also want to know a little about what happened after the incident and perhaps what the results were. This is a kind of *conclusion*. This information can also be given in a short paragraph. This paragraph comes at the end of an essay.

The following is a three-paragraph expansion of Linda's paragraph about her frightening experience. In the essay, the first paragraph tells about the *background*. The second paragraph tells about the *incident*. The third paragraph provides a *conclusion*.

> My family and I were on our way from Boston to California at the beginning of the summer. At around three o'clock in the morning, we stopped for my husband to get some sleep in a Howard Johnson's parking lot in Kansas.
> My husband and our children went to sleep, but I couldn't sleep because there was sheet lightning. Therefore, I decided to go into the Howard Johnson's for a cup of coffee. In the Howard Johnson's, there was a young man. I asked him about the sheet lightning, and he told me not to worry about it. I went back to the car. Suddenly, a terrible storm started. I woke up my husband, and he decided to continue driving. We drove to a gas station to get gas for the car. Then, things got even worse. We quickly woke up our children and began to carry and push them into the gas station. After a while, the storm stopped suddenly.
> Finally, we left the gas station and had breakfast at the Howard Johnson's. I felt relieved because the storm was over. Then, we continued on our way to California.

EXERCISE

Discuss the essay with your partner. Answer the following questions.

1. Which paragraph is the longest?
2. Why do you think it is the longest?
3. Compare the essay to the paragraph that you read in section 7. What extra information does it contain?
4. Is the extra information important? Does it tell you more about Linda's frightening experience?

Now, ask your partner to reread the paragraph that you wrote in section 7. Reread your partner's paragraph. Ask each other questions about background information and the conclusion of the incident. Write your questions for your partner. Write your answers to your partner's questions. Use your answers to expand your paragraph into a short three-paragraph essay.

9   REVISING AND EDITING

A   REVISING

Look at your partner's three-paragraph essay, and ask your partner to look at yours. Which paragraph is the longest? Is it the second paragraph? Is it the paragraph about the incident that you have written about? If not, can you help each other to change your essays to make this true? When you have finished reading the essays and helping each other, copy them over neatly and give them to each other again.

B   EDITING

Now, proofread your partner's essay, and ask your partner to proofread your essay.

1. Are the words and phrases that emphasize chronological order used correctly? Are there commas after chronological words and phrases that begin a sentence? (Review section 5A.)
2. Are adverbs of manner used correctly? Are there commas after adverbs of manner that begin a sentence? (Review section 3F.)
3. Are sentences that contain *because* and *therefore* used correctly? (Review section 5B.)

4. Are the infinitive forms correct? (Review section 3G.)
5. Are the past tense forms correct? (Review sections 3A–E.)

Write another draft of your essay on a clean piece of paper, and give it to your teacher.

10 MORE WRITING

Follow your teacher's instructions, or work on this section on your own if you have time.

1. Here is how Linda's three-paragraph essay might be expanded. The information from the original three-paragraph essay is highlighted. Use your dictionary or ask your teacher to help you with new words. Discuss the original essay and the expansion with your partner. Which one is more exciting? Why? How does the information that has been added make the longer essay more vivid? What additional information is there about the occupants of the car? about the storm? about the young man in the Howard Johnson's? about the gas station? about the writer's feelings?

There were six of us in the station wagon. **We were on our way from Boston to California**. My husband thought that motels were generally a waste of money. Because we had very little money, I didn't argue much about this. Consequently, **at around three o'clock in the morning we stopped for him to get some sleep in a Howard Johnson's parking lot in Kansas**. Our four daughters were already asleep, and he fell asleep almost immediately.
   I couldn't sleep because there was sheet lightning. For seconds at a time, it looked almost like daylight. However, the five other occupants of the station wagon continued to sleep. I became more and more nervous and found that sleep was impossible. **Therefore, I decided to go into the Howard Johnson's for a cup of coffee**. When I got there, the restaurant was almost deserted. I was the only customer. **There was a young man** who was mopping the floor. **I asked him about the sheet lightning, and he told me not to worry about it**. He said that it was caused by the heat. Because he was a native, I assumed that he knew what he was talking about. **I went back to the car**.
   Suddenly, a terrible storm started. The frequency of the sheet lightning increased, and it began to rain quite hard. At the same time, a strong wind began to blow. **I**

immediately **woke up my husband**. For some reason, **he decided to continue driving**. Because there was **a gas station** on the other side of the parking lot, **we drove to it in order to get gas for the car**.

   Then, things got even worse. The wind speed was very great, and the rain was so heavy that we could see nothing outside of the car. **We quickly woke up our children and began to carry and push them into the gas station**. Although my husband was normally quite strong, it took two of us to close the station wagon door because the wind was so strong.

   All of us were frightened. I think that we two adults were even more frightened than the children. We joined a worried teenager who was desperately trying to reach his grandfather by phone. He wanted to know if his grandfather was safe, and he was quite worried when he could not get through. The phone lines were down. Because he was a native, I asked him what to expect. He said that he didn't know. I can still remember his frightened words: "I've been living here all my life, and I've never seen anything like this before." He also told us that the gas station didn't have a cellar. Ironically, the Howard Johnson's did.

   We continued our nervous conversation for what seemed to be a century. **After a while, the storm stopped suddenly**.

   We left the gas station and had breakfast at the Howard Johnson's. The restaurant was now quite full. **I felt relieved**. After breakfast, **we continued on our way to California**. The radio spoke of fallen trees. Markings on the tree trunks provided evidence of "tornadic winds." No one on the radio called the storm a tornado, but if it wasn't one it's as close to one as I ever want to experience.

You can expand your essay even more by repeating the process of having your partner write questions that ask for more information. Just as you did before, you can begin by writing short answers to the questions. Then, you can add the information to your three-paragraph essay to make it longer and more informative.

2. Write an essay about a dream that you have had. In your conclusion, tell the reader why you think you had the dream and what it meant to you.

3. Interview a classmate or your teacher about an exciting, frightening, or dangerous experience that he or she has had. Write an essay about that person's experience. Then, show the essay to the person. Ask him or her to add information to the essay. Then, rewrite the essay.

8

Using Comparison and Contrast

Topic: Comparing places

Rhetorical Focus: Comparison and contrast

Mechanical Focus: Writing an informal outline

Grammatical Focus: Comparative forms of adjectives and adverbs; comparisons of nouns; *less/fewer*; negative comparisons; *the same as* and *as* _____ *as*

Connectors and Transitions: Marking examples with ordinal numbers and *another*

1 PRE-WRITING: READING ABOUT TWO CITIES

Lee is from Washington, D.C., but he is studying and living in Ottawa now. Here is a paragraph that he wrote about the two cities.

    There are many differences between Ottawa and Washington, D.C. For example, the climates of the two cities are different from each other. Washington is usually warmer than Ottawa, especially in the winter. There are also more black and Hispanic people in Washington than in Ottawa. However, I think that the similarities between the two cities are more important than their differences. They are similar to

each other in many important ways, so I feel as comfortable
in Ottawa as I did in Washington.

Discuss Lee's paragraph with your partner. Answer the following questions.

1. Are there any differences between Ottawa and Washington, D.C.?
2. Which differences does Lee mention?
3. Are there any similarities? How do you know?
4. Does Lee mention any of the similarities?
5. Are the similarities or the differences more important to Lee? How do you know?
6. What other information would you like to have from Lee about Ottawa and Washington, D.C.?

2 WRITING SENTENCES

**Write complete sentences to answer the following questions. Show
your partner your answers.**

1. What city or town are you in now?

   _____

2. What city or town are you from? *(If this is the same as the place you are in now,
   name a city or town that you have visited or would like to visit.)*

   _____

3. How long did you live there?

   _____

4. Name three ways in which the two places are similar to each other.

   (a) _____

   _____

   (b) _____

   _____

   (c) _____

   _____

5. Name three ways in which the two places are different from each other.

   (a) _____

   _____

   (b) _____

   _____

   (c) _____

6. Which do you think are more important: the similarities or the differences?

   _____

   _____

7. Why do you think so?

_____

_____

3 GRAMMAR

A USING CERTAIN WORDS AND PHRASES TO COMPARE AND CONTRAST

Study the underlined words and phrases in the following sentences.

1. There are many <u>similarities between</u> Boston and New York.

2. There are many <u>differences between</u> Boston and New York.

3. New York is <u>similar to</u> Boston in many ways.

4. New York is <u>different from</u> Boston in many ways.

5. Both cities are old <u>in comparison with</u> many other cities in the United States.

EXERCISE 1

Fill in the blanks in the following paragraph with the correct preposition. Choose from the following list:

between   to
from   with
in

There are many similarities _____ Boston and New York. For example, both cities are old _____ comparison _____ many other cities in the United States. The climates of the two cities are also similar _____ each other. However, I think that the differences _____ the two cities are more important than their similarities. They are different _____ each other in many important ways, so I feel very different when I am in these two cities.

B COMPARATIVE FORMS OF ADJECTIVES

Pattern (1)	Pattern (2)
New York is bigg**er than** Boston. Boston is pretti**er than** New York.	New York is **more** commercial **than** Boston. Boston is **more** romantic **than** New York.

Pattern (1)

Adjectives that contain only one syllable, and two-syllable adjectives that end in -*y* follow pattern (1).

There is a spelling change when -*er* is added to two-syllable adjectives, such as *pretty,* that end in -*y.* Can you write what it is? When a two-syllable adjective that ends in -*y* is made into a comparative, the letter *y* changes to the letter _____.

Pattern (2)

Most adjectives that contain two or more syllables follow pattern (2).

Comparative Forms of Irregular Adjectives

The irregular adjectives *good*, *bad*, and *far* form comparatives as follows.

The transportation system in New York is **better than** the one in Boston. (**good**)

The air in New York is **worse than** the air in Boston. (**bad**)

Boston is **farther** from Washington **than** New York is.

EXERCISE 2

Fill in the blanks in the following paragraph about Boston and New York with the correct comparative form of the adjective in parentheses.

An important difference between the two cities is their

sizes. Boston is _____ (small) than

New York. Therefore, different sections of the city are

_____ (close) to each other than in New

York. For example, in Boston, Chinatown and the theater

district are a short walk from each other. In New York, these

two sections are much _____ (far) apart.

Many people think that New York is _____

(confusing) than Boston because it is a much _____

(big) city. However, perhaps New York's transportation

system is _____ (good) than Boston's

because of the city's large size.

C COMPARATIVE FORMS OF ADVERBS OF MANNER

Comparative Forms of Adverbs That End in *-ly*
Most *adverbs of manner* end in *-ly*. These adverbs form comparatives according to pattern (2).
People in New York walk **more** quickly **than** people in Boston. Boston is developing **more** slowly **than** New York.

Comparative Forms of Regular One-Syllable Adverbs of Manner
A few adverbs of manner do not end in *-ly*. These adverbs form comparatives according to pattern (1).
On the highways, New Yorkers drive fast**er than** Bostonians. Do people in Boston work hard**er than** people in New York?

Comparative Forms of Irregular Adverbs of Manner
The irregular adverbs of manner *well* and *badly* form comparatives as follows.
Jobs in New York pay **better than** jobs in Boston. **(well)** People in New York drive **worse than** people in Boston. **(badly)**

EXERCISE 3

Fill in the blanks in the following paragraph with the correct comparative form of the adverb in parentheses.

Everything in New York seems to move _____

(fast) than in Boston. On the sidewalks, New Yorkers walk

_____ (quickly) than Bostonians. On the

highways, New Yorkers drive _____ (fast)

than Bostonians. Some people say that Boston drivers are not

very careful, but I believe that they drive _____

(slowly) and _____ (carefully) than New

York drivers.

D COMPARISONS OF NOUNS

All comparisons of nouns are formed according to pattern (2).

Fill in the blanks.

1. There are _____ people in New York _____ in Boston.

2. New York has _____ tall buildings _____ Boston does.

> **Comparative forms of nouns are used to compare numbers or amounts. Sentence (1) says that the *number* of people in New York is *greater than* the *number* of people in Boston. Sentence (2) means that the *number* of tall buildings in New York is *greater than* the *number* of tall buildings in Boston.**

Compare these two sentences.

> New York has more tall buildings than Boston.
> New York has taller buildings than Boston.

Discuss the two sentences with your partner. What is the difference in meaning between them?

_____

_____

E COMPARATIVES WITH *LESS* AND *FEWER*

> *Less* and *fewer* mean the opposite of *more*. The following pairs of sentences mean the same thing.
>
> 1. New York is **more** commercial **than** Boston.
>   Boston is **less** commercial **than** New York.
>
> 2. Boston is developing **more** slowly **than** New York.
>   New York is developing **less** slowly **than** Boston.
>
> 3. There are **more** people in New York **than** in Boston.
>   There are **fewer** people in Boston **than** in New York.
>
> 4. There is **more** traffic in New York **than** in Boston.
>   There is **less** traffic in Boston **than** in New York.

Countable and Uncountable Nouns			
Countable Noun	Sentence	Uncountable Noun	Sentence
cars	There are **fewer** cars in Boston than in New York.	**traffic**	There is **less** traffic in Boston than in New York.

Answer these questions.

1. Which word is used in comparing countable nouns?   fewer _____ less _____

2. Which word is used in comparing uncountable nouns?   fewer _____ less _____

EXERCISE 4

Ask your teacher to explain the difference between *developing countries* and *developed countries*. Then, talk with your partner. Can you think of some developing countries? How do you know that they are developing? Can you think of some developed countries? How do you know that they are developed?

Now, read each of the following sentences. Discuss them with your partner. Use your dictionary to look up the meanings of any words that you and your partner do not understand. If you cannot understand the definition in your dictionary, ask your teacher to help you. Then, rewrite each of the following sentences so that they have the same meaning. If the original sentence contains *more*, rewrite it by using *less* or *fewer*. If the original sentence contains *less* or *fewer*, rewrite it by using *more*. The first three sentences are done for you.

1. Developed countries have more commercial goods than developing countries.

   Developing countries have fewer commercial goods than developed countries.

2. Usually, there are fewer tall buildings in developing countries than in developed countries.

Usually, there are more tall buildings in developed countries than in developing

countries.

3. Industrialized countries are more developed than countries that are not industrialized.

   Countries that are not industrialized are less developed than industrial countries.

4. Usually, there are more cars in developed countries than in developing countries.

   _____

   _____

5. Sometimes, the air in developing countries is less polluted than the air in developed countries.

   _____

   _____

6. Usually, in developing countries, fewer people can go to college than in developed countries.

   _____

   _____

7. Food often costs proportionally more money in developing countries than in developed countries.

   _____

   _____

8. Sometimes, cities in developed countries change more slowly than those in developing countries.

   _____

   _____

9. Is there more crime in developing countries than in developed countries?

   _____

   _____

10. More people live with their families in developing countries than in developed countries.

_____

_____

Do you disagree with any of the sentences? Which ones do you disagree with? Why do you disagree with them?

F ANOTHER WAY OF EXPRESSING NEGATIVE COMPARISONS

Instead of using _less_ and _fewer_, we can also use _not as_ _____ _as_. Especially with adjectives and adverbs, this expression is usually more natural than _less_. Here are some examples of sentences that have the same meaning.

---

1. New York is **bigger than** Boston.
   Boston is **not as big as** New York.

---

2. Boston is **more romantic than** New York.
   New York is **not as romantic** as Boston.

---

3. The air in New York is **worse than** the air in Boston.
   The air in Boston is **not as bad as** the air in New York.

---

4. People in New York walk **more quickly than** people in Boston.
   People in Boston do **not** walk **as quickly as** people in New York.

---

5. Jobs in New York pay **better than** jobs in Boston.
   Jobs in Boston do **not** pay **as well as** jobs in New York.

---

6. New York has **more** tall buildings **than** Boston does.
   Boston does **not** have **as many** tall buildings **as** New York does.

EXERCISE 5

**Contrast two cities or towns that your partner knows about. Ask about
differences. Use the words in parentheses in your questions. Write
long forms of your partner's answers to your questions. The first two
are done for you.**

1. (clean)

   Is New York as clean as Boston? No, it isn't.

   New York isn't as clean as Boston.

2. (tall buildings)

   Are there as many tall buildings in New York as there are in Boston? Yes, there are.

   In fact, there are more.

   There are more tall buildings in New York than there are in Boston.

3. (expensive)

   _____

   _____

   _____

4. (traffic)

   _____

   _____

   _____

5. (noisy)

   _____

   _____

   _____

6. (crowded)

_____

_____

_____

_____

7. (quickly)

_____

_____

_____

_____

8. (developed)

_____

_____

_____

_____

9. (cost)

_____

_____

_____

_____

10. (crime)

_____

_____

_____

_____

G USING *THE SAME AS* AND *AS* _____ *AS* TO SHOW SIMILARITIES

Using *the same as* to Show Similarities Between Nouns
Read these two sentences that contain *the same as*.
New York's climate is about **the same as** Boston's climate. New York is almost **the same** age **as** Boston.

Answer these questions.

1. What is the writer comparing in each sentence?

   _____ and _____

2. What parts of speech are being compared? _____

Using *as* _____ *as* to Show Similarities with Adjectives and Adverbs
Read these two sentences that contain *as* _____ *as*.
The summer in Boston is **as** hot **as** the summer in New York. People in Boston work **as** hard **as** people in New York.

Answer these questions.

1. What part of speech is the writer comparing in the first sentence?

   _____

2. What part of speech is being compared in the second sentence?

   _____

EXERCISE 6

Ask your teacher to explain the following words.

NOUN	ADJECTIVE
city	urban
countryside	rural
suburb	suburban

Where are you from? Where is your partner from? Is your home in a city, a suburb, or the countryside? Is the place you come from urban, suburban, or rural? Do you know about other kinds of places?

Now, read the following sentences. Discuss them with your partner. Use your dictionary to look up the meanings of any words that you and your partner do not understand. If you cannot understand the definition in your dictionary, ask your teacher to help you. Then, expand each of the sentences by writing another sentence that contains a form of the word in parentheses. Use *the same as* or *as _____ as* in your sentence. The first three are done for you.

1. New York is a city, and Boston is too.

   (atmosphere) _Therefore, the atmosphere in Boston is as urban as the atmosphere in New York._

2. People in suburbs can often use the same services as people in cities.

   (convenient) _In fact, life in suburbs is often as convenient as life in cities._

3. In the United States, trucks and trains transport food from one place to another quickly.

   (food) _Therefore, people in cities and suburbs can usually eat the same kinds of food as people in the countryside._

4. Children in different parts of the United States often study similar subjects in school.

   (books) _____

5. There are beautiful things to see in both cities and the countryside.

(scenery) _____

_____

6. Clothing costs about the same in different parts of the United States.

(expensive) _____

_____

7. The pace of life in suburbs and the countryside is slower than the pace of life in cities.

(walk) _____

_____

8. It is fairly easy to find a job in both cities and suburbs.

(jobs) _____

_____

9. There are a lot of stores in cities and in suburbs.

(developed) _____

_____

10. National television companies broadcast to all parts of the United States.

(television programs) _____

_____

4 EDITING

Proofread the sentences that your partner wrote in section 2. Ask your partner to proofread your sentences.

1. Are the words and phrases used for comparison and contrast correct? Are they used with the correct prepositions? (Review section 3A.)
2. Are the comparative forms used correctly? (Review sections 3B, 3C, and 3D.)

3. Are negative comparisons expressed correctly? (Review sections 3E and 3F.)
4. Are *the same as* and *as* _____ *as* used correctly? (Review section 3G.)

After your partner proofreads your sentences, copy them correctly and give them to your teacher.

5 CONNECTORS AND TRANSITIONS

ORDINAL NUMBERS AND *ANOTHER*

In his paragraph about Washington, D.C., and Ottawa, Lee did not mention any of the similarities between the two cities. However, in the following short paragraph, he gives three of them.

> I can think of three important similarities between Washington and Ottawa. The first is that both of them are in North America. Another similarity is that English is the main language in both cities. Therefore, almost everybody can understand me when I speak. The third is that both cities are the capitals of their countries.

Underline these words and phrases in the paragraph: *the first*; *another*; and *the third*.

Another and ordinal numbers (*first, second, third, . . .*) can be used to mark separate items in a list. In Lee's paragraph, they are used to mark different examples of similarities between Washington and Ottawa.

EXERCISE

Fill in the blanks in the following paragraph with *another* or an appropriate ordinal number.

When I think about Boston and New York, three major

differences come to mind. _____ is that

New York is bigger than Boston. _____ is

the differences in the buildings in the two cities. New York's

buildings are much higher than those in Boston. _____

_____ difference is that the pace of New York is much

faster than that of Boston.

6 GETTING READY TO WRITE A PARAGRAPH

A EMPHASIZING SIMILARITIES OR DIFFERENCES

EXERCISE

Reread Lee's paragraph about Washington, D.C., and Ottawa in section 1. Then, work with your partner to put the following sentences in the correct order to make a good paragraph that emphasizes similarities. Then, copy the sentences in correct paragraph form. Show your paragraph to your teacher.

1. However, I think that the similarities between the two cities are more important than their differences.
2. The sizes of the two cities are also different from each other.
3. There are many differences between Boston and New York.
4. They are similar to each other in ways that are very important to me.
5. For example, the people and cars in New York move more quickly than those in Boston.
6. Therefore, I feel equally at home in both cities.

B ORGANIZING A PARAGRAPH ABOUT A DIFFERENCE

Reread the following paragraph that was completed in section 3C, exercise 3. It is about an important difference between Boston and New York. Discuss the paragraph with your partner. Answer the questions that follow.

Everything in New York seems to move faster than in Boston. On the sidewalks, New Yorkers walk more quickly than Bostonians. On the highways, New Yorkers drive faster than Bostonians. Some people say that Boston drivers are not very careful, but I believe that they drive more slowly and more carefully than New York drivers.

1. What is the main idea of the paragraph?
   (a) Boston drivers are more careful than New York drivers.
   (b) New Yorkers walk more quickly than Bostonians.
   (c) Everything in New York seems to move faster than in Boston.
   (d) The highways in Boston are older than those in New York.

2. Which of these statements does *not* support the main idea?
   (a) New Yorkers walk more quickly than Bostonians.
   (b) Bostonians drive faster than New Yorkers.
   (c) On the highways, New Yorkers drive faster than Bostonians.
   (d) Bostonians drive more slowly than New Yorkers.

3. Which sentence in the paragraph is an example of a general statement?

   _____

   _____

4. Which sentences give examples that support this general statement?

   _____

   _____

   _____

   _____

   _____

C SIMPLE OUTLINES

Here is a simple *outline* of the paragraph in section 6B.

An important difference between Boston and New York:
Everything in New York seems to move faster than in Boston.

Examples:
   1. New Yorkers walk more quickly than Bostonians.
   2. New Yorkers drive more quickly than Bostonians.

Now, work with your partner to *outline* a paragraph about an important difference between the place you are in now and the other one that you wrote about in section 2. Perhaps you will want to write about *size*, *speed*, *age*, or *climate*. Answer the following questions. You may need to get information from your teacher or the library. When you finish your outline, show it to your teacher.

What is an important difference between the two places?

_____

_____

What are two or three examples of this difference?

1. _____
2. _____
3. _____

Now, work with your partner to write a simple outline of a paragraph about a *similarity* between the two places. Write your outline on a clean piece of paper, and give it to your teacher.

7 WRITING A PARAGRAPH

In this section, you will write five paragraphs. Write each one on a clean piece of paper.

A WRITING A PARAGRAPH THAT EMPHASIZES SIMILARITIES OR DIFFERENCES

Discuss your answers to the questions in section 2 with your partner. Explain why you think the similarities or differences between the two places are more important. Then, write a paragraph that emphasizes either similarities or differences.

Begin your paragraph by mentioning whichever you think are less important (the similarities or the differences). Give two or three examples. Then, write about whichever you think are more important. Finish your paragraph by writing about why you think these are more important.

B WRITING A PARAGRAPH ABOUT A DIFFERENCE

Now, you are going to write a paragraph based on your first outline in section 6C. Begin your paragraph with a sentence that briefly describes the difference. Follow this sentence with examples of the difference.

C WRITING ANOTHER PARAGRAPH ABOUT A DIFFERENCE

Now, look again at the answers that you wrote in section 2. Choose another difference between the two places. Discuss this difference with your partner and give several examples. Make an outline, and use it to write a paragraph.

D WRITING A PARAGRAPH ABOUT A SIMILARITY

Look at the outline that you wrote in section 6C for a paragraph about a similarity between the two places. Use it to write a paragraph. Begin your paragraph with a sentence that briefly describes the similarity. Follow this sentence with examples of the similarity.

E WRITING ANOTHER PARAGRAPH ABOUT A SIMILARITY

Now, look again at the answers that you wrote in section 2. Choose another similarity between the two places. Discuss this similarity with your partner and give several examples. Make an outline, and use it to write a paragraph.

8 EXPANDING YOUR PARAGRAPHS

A A FIVE-PARAGRAPH COMPARISON AND CONTRAST ESSAY

The following is a five-paragraph essay about some of the differences between Boston and New York.

Differences Between Boston and New York

There are many similarities between Boston and New York. For example, both cities are old in comparison with many other cities in the United States. The climates of the two cities are also similar to each other. However, I think that the differences between the two cities are more important than their similarities. They are different from each other in many important ways, so I feel very different when I am in these two cities.

An important difference between the two cities is their sizes. Boston is smaller than New York. Therefore, different sections of the city are closer to each other than in New York. For example, in Boston, Chinatown and the theater district are a short walk from each other. In New York, these two sections are much farther apart. Many people think that New York is more confusing than Boston because it is a much bigger city. However, perhaps New York's transportation system is better than Boston's because of the city's large size.

Another difference is the height of the buildings in the two cities. When people think of New York, they often think of its skyline. The city's tall buildings have made it famous. When you drive into the city, this is the first thing that you notice. People from all over the world expect to see the Empire State Building, although this is no longer the tallest building in the world. Boston also has some skyscrapers, but none of them is as tall as those in New York. Although the John Hancock Building and the Prudential Tower dominate the Boston skyline, they are not as high as many of the buildings in New York.

A third important difference is the pace of New York and Boston. Everything in New York seems to move faster than in Boston. On the sidewalks, New Yorkers walk more quickly than Bostonians. On the highways, New Yorkers drive faster than Bostonians. Some people say that Boston drivers are not very careful, but I believe that they drive more slowly and more carefully than New York drivers.

The different atmospheres of Boston and New York are shown by their size, buildings, and pace. Boston and New York are both important cities in the northeastern United States. They have many similarities, but their differences are more important.

B OUTLINING AN ESSAY

The following is an outline of the essay in section 8A.

1. *Introduction*: The differences between Boston and New York are more important than their similarities.
2. *First Difference*: Size
   Examples:
   (a) Boston is smaller than New York.
   (b) Different sections of Boston are closer to each other.
   (c) New York may have a better transportation system because of its larger size.
3. *Second Difference*: Buildings
   Examples:
   (a) New York's skyline is famous.
   (b) The Empire State Building is famous.
   (c) The John Hancock Building and the Prudential Tower are not as high as many of the buildings in New York.
4. *Third Difference*: Pace
   Examples:
   (a) New Yorkers walk more quickly.
   (b) New Yorkers drive faster.
5. *Conclusion*: These three differences give the cities different atmospheres.

In section 7, you wrote five paragraphs. The first one tells whether you think the similarities or the differences between two places are more important. You can use this paragraph as the introduction to your essay.

Based on your introduction and the answers that you wrote in section 2, outline a five-paragraph essay about the two places. Write your outline on a clean piece of paper.

C WRITING A FIVE-PARAGRAPH ESSAY THAT EMPHASIZES SIMILARITIES OR DIFFERENCES

Now, use your outline and some of the paragraphs that you wrote in section 7 to write a five-paragraph essay about the two places.

9 REVISING AND EDITING

A REVISING

Read your partner's outline and five-paragraph essay. Let your partner read your outline and essay. Answer the following questions.

1. Do the outline and the essay agree with each other?
2. Does the introductory paragraph tell you what the essay is going to emphasize?
3. Do the three paragraphs of the body each give one similarity or difference?
4. Does the conclusion mention the three items from the body of the essay?

Ask your partner questions about anything that you do not understand. Ask for more information if you think it is necessary. Answer any questions that your partner has about your outline or essay.

After you discuss your essay with your partner, make any changes that you think are necessary. Then, copy the essay onto a clean piece of paper.

B EDITING

Now, proofread your partner's essay and ask your partner to proofread your essay.

1. Are the words and phrases used for comparison and contrast correct? Are they used with the correct prepositions? (Review section 3A.)
2. Are the comparative forms used correctly? (Review sections 3B–D.)
3. Are *less* and *fewer* used correctly? (Review section 3E.)
4. Are *the same as* and *as* _____ *as* used correctly? (Review sections 3F and G.)
5. Are *another* and ordinal numbers used correctly? (Review section 5.)

After your partner proofreads your essay, copy it over onto a clean piece of paper. Give your essay to your teacher.

10 MORE WRITING

Follow your teacher's instructions, or work on this section on your own if you have time.

1. Compare two people. You may compare yourself and another person in your family, two classmates, or two political leaders. You may compare any two people that you want to.
2. Compare your country's food with that of another country.
3. Compare women and men.

CHAPTER **9**

Giving Advice

Topic: Making suggestions

Rhetorical Focus: Giving advice

Mechanical Focus: Writing a friendly letter

Grammatical Focus: Verbs that are followed by infinitives; verbs that are followed by gerunds; simple modals; present and future real conditionals; superlatives

Connectors and Transitions: *on the other hand; in any case*

---

1 PRE-WRITING: DISCUSSING ALTERNATIVES

Read the following paragraph. Ask your partner or your teacher about any words that you do not understand. Then, close your book and take out a piece of paper. Your teacher will dictate the paragraph. Write the paragraph.

Karen is a high school student in Los Angeles. She is going to graduate this year, and she has to decide about her future education. She is the best violinist in her school, so she is thinking about going to a conservatory to study the violin and become a musician. On the other hand, she also understands computers very well. Therefore, her parents want her to go to a university and study computer science.

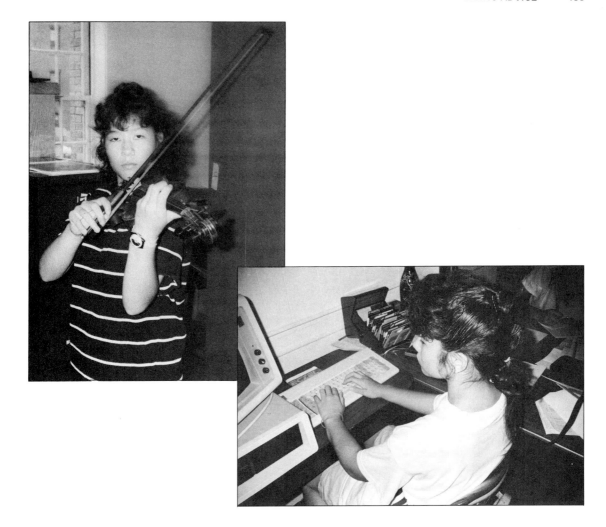

Exchange paragraphs with your partner. Proofread each other's work. Correct your work, and give your paper to your teacher.

Now, discuss Karen's problem with your partner. Here are some questions that may help you in your discussion.

1. What decision does Karen have to make?
2. What are her alternatives?
3. Will she feel happy if she does what her parents want her to do?
4. Will she be happy if she becomes a successful musician?
5. What should Karen do? Why?
6. Should young people always listen to their parents?

2 WRITING SENTENCES

Do you have to make a decision? Does your partner? Ask each other questions about the decisions that you have to make. Write your questions about your partner's decision.

My Questions About the Decision
That My Partner Has to Make

_____

_____

_____

_____

_____

_____

_____

_____

_____

_____

_____

Now, write answers to your partner's questions. Show your answers to your partner.

My Answers to My Partner's
Questions About the Decision
That I Have to Make

_____

_____

_____

_____

_____

_____

_____

3 GRAMMAR

A   VERBS THAT ARE FOLLOWED BY INFINITIVES AND VERBS THAT ARE FOLLOWED BY GERUNDS

You have already begun to study verbs that are followed by infinitives in Chapter 7. Now, look at the following pairs of sentences.

Noun Object	Infinitive
Karen wants a **new violin**.	Karen wants **to study**.
Noun Object	**Gerund**
Karen enjoys **music**.	Karen enjoys **singing**.

Fill in the blanks.

1. Infinitives and gerunds can take the same place in a sentence as a

   _____ _____.

2. What three letters come at the end of a gerund? _____.

EXERCISE 1

Some verbs are followed by infinitives, and others are followed by gerunds. Read the following paragraph. Underline the phrases that

contain verbs that are followed by infinitives. Circle the phrases that contain verbs that are followed by gerunds. Then, make a list of each kind of verb. Two are done for you.

Karen <u>started to play</u> the violin when she was four years old. This was before she learned to read music. In fact, it was before she learned to read. She (enjoyed playing) the violin so much that her kindergarten teacher advised her parents to give her violin lessons. They decided to send her for lessons once a week. They encouraged her to play the violin, but they always expected her to be a good student. They appreciated hearing her play the violin. She really enjoyed it. When she finished practicing, she often didn't want to stop. She kept playing the violin.

Verbs That Are Followed by Infinitives	Verbs That Are Followed by Gerunds
start	enjoy

You can continue this list in your notebook. When you are reading and you see a verb that is followed by an infinitive or a gerund, add it to your list.

> **Some verbs that are followed by the infinitive take an object that comes before the infinitive. Here are some examples.**
>
> 1. Karen's parents expect **her** to study.
> 2. Karen's teacher encouraged **her** to play the violin.

In these sentences, the object that comes before the infinitive functions like the subject of the infinitive. Each sentence can be seen as coming from two sentences.

1. Karen's parents expect that.

   She should study.

   Karen's parents expect *her* to study.

2. Karen's teacher encouraged that.

   She should play the violin.

   Karen's teacher encouraged *her* to play the violin.

EXERCISE 2

Combine each pair of sentences to make one sentence that contains a verb that takes an object followed by an infinitive.

1. Karen asked her parents.

   They should pay for her violin lessons.

   _____

   _____

2. Her parents want that.

   She should study hard.

   _____

   _____

3. Her teacher urged that.

She should practice every day.

_____

_____

4. Her teacher expects that.

She will be a good violinist.

_____

_____

EXERCISE 3

Answer the following questions about yourself. Write complete sentences.

1. What do you want to do when you graduate?

_____

_____

2. What do your parents, friends, or relatives want you to do?

_____

_____

3. What do you enjoy studying?

_____

_____

4. What kind of music do you appreciate hearing?

_____

_____

5. Who encouraged you to study English?

_____

_____

B PRESENT AND FUTURE SIMPLE MODALS

The present and future simple modals are:

can	must
may	should
might	will

EXERCISE 4

Read the following paragraph about Karen, and underline the simple modals and the verbs that follow them. One is done for you.

Karen has to make her decision before she graduates from high school. She <u>must decide</u> where she will study after that. Her friends think that she should talk with her guidance counselor. The counselor can ask her questions and make suggestions. They say that the counselor may help her to decide what to do. He will not make the decision for her, but she might be able to make her decision more easily after she talks to him.

Answer the following questions.

1. What form of the verb do simple modals come before?

   _____

2. Do they change their form according to the subject of the sentence?

   yes _____ no _____

3. What word occurs between a simple modal and the verb to make a negative? _____

EXERCISE 5

Rewrite each of the following sentences to contain the modal in parentheses. Do not change the basic meaning of the sentence. The first two are done for you.

1. It is possible that Karen is going to take her parents' advice. (may)

   Karen may take her parents' advice.

2. It is a good idea for Karen to find out more about being a musician. (should)

   Karen should find out more about being a musician.

3. It is possible for Karen to study the violin while she is in college. (can)

   _____

   _____

4. It is necessary for Karen to really think about what she is going to do. (must)

   _____

   _____

5. It is a good idea for Karen's parents to let her make her own decision. (should)

   _____

   _____

6. Karen is going to feel better if she talks to her guidance counselor. (will)

   _____

   _____

C   PRESENT AND FUTURE REAL CONDITIONALS

Read the following conversation between Karen and her friend Carl.

Carl: What's the matter, Karen? You look unhappy.

Karen: I'm not unhappy, I'm just confused. I want to go to college, but I also want to study the violin.

Carl: Can't you study the violin if you go to college?

Karen: Yes, I guess I can, but I'll also have to spend time studying for my college classes. If I don't study the violin full-time, I won't ever become a professional violinist.

Carl: You have a real problem. The best thing is to make an appointment with Mr. McBride. If you tell him about it, he may have some ideas.

Answer these questions.

1. What is the contraction form for *will*? _____

2. What is the contraction for *will not*? _____

We do not always know what is happening in the present; we do not know what is going to happen in the future. However, we can think about what *may* happen and talk about the results *if* this happens. For this purpose, we use real conditional sentences.

In a real conditional sentence, the *if*-clause tells what we think is happening or is going to happen. The result clause tells what we think the result is or will be.

If-clause	Result Clause
If Karen really **likes** to play the violin,	she should go to a conservatory.
If Karen **speaks** with her counselor,	he will help her.

Answer these questions.

1. What is the tense of the verb in the *if*-clause? _____

2. What punctuation mark is used after the *if*-clause? _____

EXERCISE 6

Reread the conversation between Karen and Carl on pages 202 and 203. Underline the conditional sentences. Draw a circle around the main verb in the *if*-clause in each sentence.

EXERCISE 7

Use the information in each situation to write present or future real conditional sentences. The first two sentences are done for you.

1. Karen should talk with Mr. McBride. He usually gives students good advice.

   If Karen talks with Mr. McBride, he will probably give her good advice.

2. Karen may study at the conservatory. Then, she will become a professional violinist.

   If Karen studies at the conservatory, she will become a professional violinist.

3. Karen may just study the violin in her spare time. Then, she will probably not become a professional violinist.

4. Karen's parents want her to go to college. Then, they will be happy.

_____

_____

5. Sometimes, people need to discuss their problems with someone. Then, they should speak with their friends.

_____

_____

> **Conditional sentences do not have to begin with the *if*-clause. The *if*-clause may come last. Then, there is no comma.**

EXERCISE 8

Rewrite the sentences that you wrote in exercise 7. Put the *if*-clause last.

1. _Mr. McBride will probably give Karen good advice if she talks with him._

2. _____

_____

3. _____

_____

4. _____

_____

5. _____

_____

D SUPERLATIVES

Superlative forms show that a person or thing has more of a quality than anyone or anything else in a group. Here are some examples.

Karen is *the best* violinist in her school.
(This sentence means that Karen is a better violinist than anyone else in her school.)

The best thing for Karen is to talk to Mr. McBride.
(This sentence means that it is better for Karen to talk to Mr. McBride than to do anything else.)

Karen is *the oldest* child in her family.
(This sentence means that Karen is older than any of the other children in her family.)

Comparative and Superlative Forms	
Comparative Form	**Sentence Containing the Superlative Form**
young**er**	Carl is **the youngest** person in his class.
bett**er**	Mr. McBride is **the best** guidance counselor in the school.
worse	**The worst** thing Karen can do is to quit school after she graduates.
less	History is **the least** interesting class for Karen.
more	It is **the most** interesting class for Carl.
few**er**	Karen's advanced computer science class has **the fewest** students of all her classes.

Answer these questions.

1. What word comes before a superlative form? _____

2. When the comparative form ends in *-er*, what letters does the superlative

form end in? _____

3. What *two* letters do *all* superlative forms end in? _____

EXERCISE 9

Rewrite each comparative sentence as a sentence that contains a superlative form. Be sure that you keep the meaning of the original sentence.

1. History is more interesting to Carl than any other subject.

   History is the most interesting subject to Carl.

2. Carl is a better French student than any of his classmates.

   Carl is the best French student in his class.

3. Karen's music teacher is younger than any of the other teachers in the school.

   _____

   _____

4. Science is less interesting to Carl than any of his other subjects.

   _____

   _____

5. Carl's French class has fewer students than any of his other classes.

   _____

   _____

6. For Karen to be happy is more important than anything else.

   Being happy is _____

   _____

7. The day that her parents told her not to go to a conservatory was worse than any other day in Karen's life.

   _____

   _____

4 EDITING

Proofread the sentences that your partner wrote in section 2, and ask your partner to proofread your sentences. Check the following.

1. Are infinitive and gerund forms used correctly? (Review section 3A.)
2. Are modals used correctly? Are they followed by the simple form of the verb? (Review section 3B.)
3. Are real conditionals used correctly? Is the *if*-clause in the present tense? (Review section 3C.)
4. Are superlative forms used correctly? (Review section 3D.)

5 CONNECTORS AND TRANSITIONS

A ON THE OTHER HAND

On the other hand **is used to show a contrast.**

Karen may be happy if she studies the violin. *On the other hand,* she may also be happy if she studies computer science.

Karen's parents know that she will enjoy studying the violin. *On the other hand,* they think that she will be more successful if she goes to college.

B IN ANY CASE

In any case **is used when the result will be the same regardless of what happens.**

Karen may study the violin, or she may study computer science. *In any case,* she will not stop studying when she finishes high school.

Mr. McBride may have some good ideas for Karen, or he may just listen to her talk about her problems. *In any case,* she will feel better if she talks to him.

Fill in the blanks.

1. Both *on the other hand* and *in any case* come at the beginning of a

    _____ .

2. Both phrases are followed by a _____ .

EXERCISE

Read the following sentences about pollution and energy. Use your dictionary to look up words that you do not understand. Ask your partner or your teacher for help if you do not understand the definitions. Then, fill in each blank with *on the other hand* or *in any case*. Then, copy the sentences in the space provided. Be sure to punctuate correctly.

1. Cars have advantages and disadvantages. They make traveling easier.

    _____ , they cause air pollution.

    _____

    _____

    _____

2. We may develop solar and nuclear energy in the future, or we may continue to

    depend on oil. _____ , our energy needs are

    not going to decrease.

    _____

    _____

    _____

3. Many people say that nuclear energy is dangerous. _____

    _____ , some people point out that it does not pollute the atmosphere like oil

    and coal.

_____

_____

_____

4. We should work to develop cleaner forms of energy. _____

_____ , we also have to worry about how much our energy will cost.

_____

_____

_____

Do you disagree with any of the sentences? Which ones do you disagree with? Why do you disagree with them?

6 GETTING READY TO WRITE A PARAGRAPH

Reread the paragraph about Karen's problems in section 1. The information in the paragraph can be put into an outline like the following one.

  I. *Decision:* Karen is going to graduate from high school this year, and she has to decide about her future education.

 II. *Alternatives:*

   A. She is thinking about going to a school where she can study the violin and become a musician because she is an excellent violinist.

   B. Her parents want her to go to a university and study computer science because she also understands computers very well.

Now, reread the answers that your partner wrote to your questions in section 2. Let your partner reread your answers. Answer the following questions.

  1. What decisions does your partner have to make?
  2. What are the alternatives?

Fill in the following outline with information from your partner's answers. Use complete sentences. Let your partner make an outline based on your answers.

A Decision

I. Decision: _____

_____

_____

II. Alternatives:

A. _____

_____

B. _____

_____

7 WRITING A PARAGRAPH

Now, use your outline to write a paragraph about the decision that your partner has to make. When you have finished your first draft, show it to your partner to see if the information is accurate. Then, make any changes that are necessary.

8 EXPANDING YOUR PARAGRAPH

A THE FORM OF A FRIENDLY LETTER

Karen and Carl spoke with each other right before a school vacation. Carl went out of town with his family for the vacation, so he didn't see Karen. However, he thought about her problem. He decided to write her a letter and give her some advice. This is what he wrote.

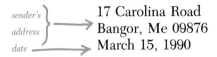

sender's address } ⟶ 17 Carolina Road
                        Bangor, Me 09876
date ⟶ March 15, 1990

Ms. Karen Park
1238 East Elm Street ⟵ { *recipient's name and address*
Los Angeles, CA 90035

Dear Karen, ⟵ *salutation*   *body of the letter* ↓

I know that you have a problem. You are going to graduate from high
school this year, and you have to decide about your future education. You
are the best violinist in our school, and you are thinking about going to a
conservatory because you can study the violin there and become a musician.
On the other hand, you are also very good with computers, and your parents
want you to go to a university and study computer science. This is a real
problem because your decision will affect your future.

I think that you should go to the conservatory. If you don't study the violin
now, you won't be able to play it very well when you get older. If you don't
like the conservatory, you can always change your mind and go to college. A
lot of students start studying in college when they are older, but it is
important to study a musical instrument when you are young.

At first, your parents may be unhappy if you decide not to go to the
university. However, you can talk to them and give them your reasons. If you
talk to them maturely, they may trust your decision. In any case, it's your
life, not theirs.

I hope that you don't mind my giving you advice. I dreamed about you
last night. I saw you playing the violin in a computer laboratory. The violin
didn't sound very good, and the computers kept breaking. When I woke up,
I thought that you had to make a decision as soon as possible. I decided to
write this letter to you and give you my opinion. Now, I think that I can
sleep well tonight.

I hope this letter will help you to reach your decision. You don't have to
listen to me, but at least you have a definite opinion to think about.

Have a good vacation. I'll see you next week.

closing ⟶ Sincerely,

signature ⟶ *Carl*

Read Carl's letter to Karen. Answer the following questions.

1. Which side of the page is the sender's (Carl's) address on?

    the right side _____   the left side _____

2. Whose name and address start at the left margin? _____

3. Is Karen the sender or the recipient of the letter? _____

4. Where is the date? _____

5. What is the salutation? _____

    Where does it begin? _____

    What punctuation mark comes after the salutation? _____

6. What is the closing? _____

    What side of the page is it on? _____

    What punctuation mark comes after the closing? _____

7. Where is the signature? _____

B ADDRESSING AN ENVELOPE

Here is how the envelope that Carl used to mail his letter to Karen looked.

Carl Powell
17 Carolina Road
Bangor, ME 09876

Ms. Karen Park
1238 East Elm Street
Los Angeles, CA 90035

Answer these questions.

    1. Where is the sender's (Carl's) address? _____

    2. Where is the recipient's (Karen's) address? _____

C   WRITING A FRIENDLY LETTER OF ADVICE

Reread your paragraph about your partner's decision. Then, on a clean piece of paper, write a letter to your partner. Summarize the problem and say what decision you think he or she should make. Address an envelope for the letter.

9   REVISING AND EDITING

A   REVISING

    1. Does your letter summarize your partner's problem?
    2. Do you make suggestions for your partner?
    3. Make additions that you think are necessary. Then, copy your letter over onto a clean piece of paper.

B   EDITING

Reread your letter to your partner.

    1. (a) Does it contain the following items?

            your address   a salutation
            the date   a closing
            your partner's name and address
            your signature

       (b) Are they in the correct places? (Look at Carl's letter on page 212.)
    2. Are modals and real conditionals used correctly? (Review sections 3B and C.)
    3. Are infinitive and gerund forms correct? (Review section 3A.)
    4. Are superlative forms used correctly? (Review section 3D.)
    5. Are *on the other hand* and *in any case* used correctly? (Review section 5.)

Look at the envelope that you addressed.

1. Is your address in the correct place?
2. Is your partner's address in the correct place? (Look at Carl's envelope on page 213.)

Make any necessary corrections. Then, put the letter into the envelope and give it to your partner. Read your partner's letter to you.

10 MORE WRITING

Follow your teacher's instructions, or work on this section on your own if you have time.

1. Read another classmate's description of his or her partner's problem. Then, write a letter of advice to that person.
2. Answer your partner's letter about the decision that you have to make.
3. Write a short essay about a problem in your country or the world. For example, you may want to write about pollution, energy, or food. Begin your essay by describing the problem. Then give two or more possible solutions. Briefly tell what you think will happen if these solutions are tried. Finally, say what you think the best solution is and why you think so.

CHAPTER 10

Writing About the Past

Topic: Describing childhood events

Rhetorical Focus: Giving background information; narrowing the focus to a specific incident

Mechanical Focus: Quotation marks

Grammatical Focus: Past continuous tense; *while*; *used to*

Connectors and Transitions: *although*

1 PRE-WRITING: MAKING INFERENCES

Read the following paragraph about a day in Linda's childhood. Use your dictionary to look up any new vocabulary, or ask your teacher about it.

When I was in the second grade, Easter came in March. We were on my grandparents' farm in Florida, and my teacher came to visit. Although it was raining lightly, my brother, cousin, and I were hunting Easter eggs. I didn't expect my teacher to come. I was walking around looking for eggs when I heard a car. It was hers! I was thrilled. My teacher was visiting us on Easter Sunday. While I was hugging her, my mother, grandparents, and uncle came out to greet her more formally. She had presents for us three children. I was so happy that I didn't mind her giving candy and Easter eggs to my brother and cousin. It was one of the best days of my childhood.

Work with your partner. Answer the following questions about the paragraph.

1. About how old was Linda? How do you know?
2. How did she feel? What sentences tell you this?
3. Which word best describes how Linda felt about her teacher?

   (a) unhappy   (c) possessive
   (b) formal   (d) disinterested

   What sentence gives you this idea?

2 WRITING SENTENCES

Ask your partner the following questions, and let your partner ask you the same questions. Write down your answers to your partner's questions.

1. What was one of the most important days of your childhood?

   _____

   _____

2. About how old were you?

_____

_____

3. Where were you?

_____

_____

4. How did you feel?

_____

_____

5. What happened?

_____

_____

3 GRAMMAR

A THE PAST CONTINUOUS TENSE

The Past Continuous Tense		
Subject	**Past Continuous**	**Rest of the Sentence**
I	was walking	around.
You	were living	in Florida.
He	was greeting	her.
She	was getting	out of her car.
It	was raining	lightly.
We	were hunting	Easter eggs.
You	were hugging	each other.
They	were visiting.	

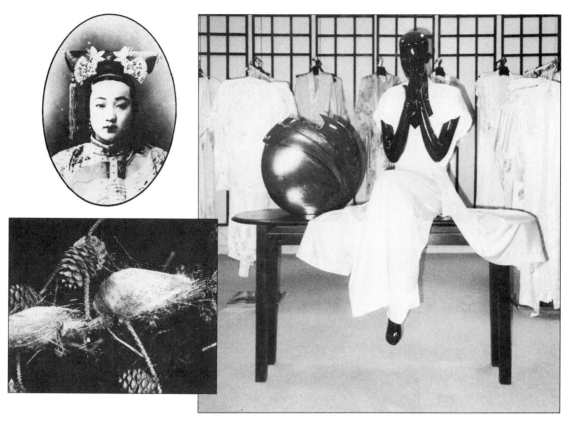

Answer these questions.

1. Is the past continuous similar to the present continuous?

   yes _____   no _____

2. What tense of the verb *to be* does it contain? _____

According to legend, a Chinese empress discovered silk. These sentences tell how some people think silk was discovered.

1. The empress sat in her garden all morning.
   (a) A cocoon dropped from a mulberry tree.
   (b) It fell into her tea cup.
   (c) It unwound into a long filament.
2. She hung the filament up to dry.
3. It was drying.
   (a) She soaked other cocoons.
   (b) She hung up the filaments.
4. She wove the filaments into beautiful cloth.

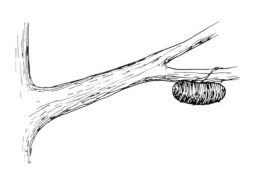

EXERCISE 1

Work with your partner. Fill in the blanks in the following paragraph with the correct *past continuous* form of the verb in parentheses. Then, copy the paragraph onto a clean piece of paper, and give it to your teacher.

Some people say that a Chinese empress discovered silk

while she _____

(sit) in her garden. She _____

_____ (drink) a cup of tea when a cocoon from a

mulberry tree fell into her tea cup. The hot tea softened the

cocoon, and a long silk filament unwound. She took the

filament out of her cup and hung it up to dry. While it

_____ (dry), she

soaked other cocoons and hung them up. When they were

dry, she wove them into a beautiful cloth.

B THE PAST CONTINUOUS TENSE AND THE SIMPLE PAST TENSE: *WHEN* AND *WHILE*

Both the past continuous and the simple past are used to talk or write about past events. Look at the sentences on page 219. Then, look at the sentences in the paragraph that you copied in exercise 1. Pay special attention to the sentences that contain both tenses.

In these sentences, the past continuous is used for events that were *longer* than the events that are described by using the simple past.

EXERCISE 2

Now, read the paragraph in section 1 again. Underline the sentences that contain both tenses. Discuss them with your partner. Why is the past continuous used?

Circle the words *when* and *while* in the paragraph. Which one is used in clauses that contain the simple past? Which one is used in clauses that contain the past continuous?

EXERCISE 3

Read the following pairs of sentences. Ask your partner about any words that you do not understand or people that you have not heard of. Look up any words and names that both of you don't understand in a dictionary. If you don't understand some of the definitions or descriptions, ask your teacher to help you.

Next, combine each pair to make one sentence that contains a past continuous verb and a simple past verb. Use *when* or *while* in your sentences. (Do not use all of the words in your combined sentence.) Be sure to use the past continuous for longer actions. The first two are done for you.

1. Isaac Newton slept under an apple tree from the morning until the afternoon. An apple fell on his head in the afternoon.

   While Isaac Newton was sleeping under an apple tree, an apple fell on his head. /

   Isaac Newton was sleeping under an apple tree when an apple fell on his head.

2. Alexander Graham Bell talked on the telephone to his assistant. During their conversation, some acid dropped on Mr. Bell's foot.

   Alexander Graham Bell was talking on the telephone to his assistant when some acid

   dropped on his foot. / While Alexander Graham Bell was talking on the telephone to

   his assistant, some acid dropped on his foot.

3. The astronauts traveled around the earth for several hours. They spoke to people on the earth for a few minutes.

   _____

   _____

4. We listened to the news all day. We heard that President Kennedy was dead.

   _____

   _____

5. The sailors stood on the deck of the ship all day. Someone sighted land in the afternoon.

_____

_____

6. President Lincoln watched a play at the theater. During the play, John Wilkes Booth shot him.

_____

_____

7. The scientist looked at the bacteria through a microscope. During this time, they began to multiply.

_____

_____

EXERCISE 4

Talk with your partner about the beginning of your class today. Try to answer these questions. Show your answers to your teacher.

1. What were you doing when your teacher came into the classroom?

_____

_____

2. What did you do when your teacher came into the classroom?

_____

_____

3. What was your partner doing then?

_____

_____

4. What did your partner do then?

_____

_____

C USED TO

Used to plus the simple form of the verb describes actions or states that occurred regularly in the past.

EXERCISE 5

Fill in the blanks in the following paragraph with *used to* plus the simple form of the verb. (You can look up unfamiliar words in your dictionary or ask your partner or teacher about them.) The first one is done for you.

Silk is an important fabric today, but in the past it _used to_

_be_ even more important. Today, we have synthetic materials

that look like silk and are easier to take care of, but until this

century silk _____ (be) the only material

that had its unique shine and texture. Merchants _____

_____ (travel) between

China and the Middle East, buy silk, and sell it for high prices.

Europeans _____ (go) to the Middle East

to buy silk and bring it back to sell at a great profit. Only

royalty and wealthy people _____

_____ (wear) clothes that were made

of silk. Although it is expensive today, people who are not

wealthy can afford it.

EXERCISE 6

Read these sentences about Linda.

1. Linda used to visit Florida every year, but she doesn't go there anymore.
2. Linda used to be a student, but now she is a teacher.

Talk with your partner. Ask each other questions about the past and now. Write three sentences about your partner that contain *used to*.

1. _____

   _____

2. _____

   _____

3. _____

   _____

D   PUNCTUATION: USING QUOTATION MARKS

> Quotation marks (") are used whenever we report someone's *exact words*. They are put at the beginning and end of the quotation. Commas and periods are put *before* closing quotation marks.

EXERCISE 7

Read the following dialogue. Then, complete the sentences that report what the speakers said. Copy your sentences onto a clean piece of paper.

Miss Brock:	Happy Easter, Jim.
Jim:	Happy Easter. It was nice of you to bring presents for the children.
Miss Brock:	Oh, it was nothing. I like to make children happy.
Jim:	Yes, I guess that's why you're a teacher.

1. Miss Brock said, __*"Happy Easter, Jim."*_____

2. Jim replied, _____

   _____

3. She answered, _____

_____

4. He said, _____

_____

EXERCISE 8

Write a short list of questions for your partner. Ask your partner to answer them in your book. Then, write sentences that report what you asked and what your partner wrote. Use quotation marks in these sentences.

Questions for My Partner

_____

_____

_____

_____

_____

_____

My Partner's Answers

_____

_____

_____

_____

_____

What I Asked, and
What My Partner Answered

I asked my partner,   " _____ ?"

My partner answered,   " _____ ."

_____

_____

_____

_____

_____

4 EDITING

**Let your partner proofread the sentences that you wrote in section 2.
Proofread your partner's sentences.**

1. Are the forms of the past continuous correct? (Review section 3A.)
2. Are *when* and *while* used correctly? (Review section 3B.)
3. Is *used to* used correctly? (Review section 3C.)

Correct your sentences, and give them to your teacher.